100 ACTIVITIES

Based on the

Catechism of the Catholic Church

Second Edition

ELLEN ROSSINI

FOR GRADES 1 TO 8

IGNATIUS PRESS   SAN FRANCISCO

Illustrations on pages 18, 19, 20, and 32 by John Herreid and Moira Farrell.

Cover design by Riz Boncan Marsella

Revised Edition
ISBN 978-1-58617-795-9

© 2013 Ignatius Press, San Francisco
Permission granted to reproduce student material for classroom use only.
All other rights reserved.

Printed by Thomson-Shore, Dexter, MI (USA); RMA 596JM406, July, 2014.
In compliance with the Consumer Protection Safety Act of 2008.

Contents

Introduction

Occasionally in preparing a lesson, a religion teacher needs an extra activity—a short worksheet or a more involved classroom exercise—to convey a message of faith or point of doctrine. At other times, even with good planning, a teacher needs a productive way to engage students for the last 10 or 15 minutes of a class period.

This book was created to help teachers meet these needs. Designed as a supplement for any Catholic catechetical program, it draws its format and content from the *Catechism of the Catholic Church*. The *Catechism* was affirmed by Pope John Paul II "to be a sure norm for teaching the faith" and an "authentic reference text for teaching catholic doctrine and particularly for preparing local catechisms" (*Fidei Depositum*, 1992).

This second edition, published during the twentieth year of the *Catechism*, incorporates changes in the prayers of the Mass and Nicene Creed from the 2011 revised English translation of the Roman Missal, as well as other changes since the first publication, such as the addition of the Luminous Mysteries of the Rosary. New activities have replaced some of the original ones, and related exercises have been combined into a single activity with two or more options.

The classroom activities in this book are numbered 1 through 100 and are arranged into three skill levels: primary (grades 1–3), intermediate (grades 3–5), and advanced (grades 6–8). Some primary activities may be appropriate for intermediate students, intermediate for advanced, or advanced for intermediate, depending on the students.

Each activity is self-contained and reproducible for classroom use. Few additional materials are required, though student Bibles are often necessary. Most lessons require little advance preparation by the teacher, and most can be completed well within a class period.

Activities for the class as a whole, such as games and discussions, include step-by-step instructions for the teacher. Individual student activities consist of a brief introductory lesson or explanation for the student and an exercise to be completed by the student on his own. The student activities range from simple matchings, fill-in-the-blanks, and multiple-choice questions to more involved Bible research, short answers, and essays. Some exercises may be suitable as tests or review assignments, others as homework or research projects.

The topics of the activities are organized according to the four pillars of the *Catechism*:
> The Profession of Faith
> The Celebration of the Christian Mystery
> Life in Christ
> Christian Prayer

At the top of the page of each activity are the citations of the paragraphs in the *Catechism* (abbreviated CCC) that apply to the lesson. This valuable reference enables teachers to review key doctrinal points as a background for each activity. It is recommended that teachers have easy access to a copy of the *Catechism* and that those teaching older students have an extra copy to make available to the class. Besides being a vital tool for catechetical instruction, the *Catechism* is a beautiful and uplifting summary of our Catholic faith and is "useful reading for all . . . Christian faithful" (CCC 12).

Naturally, 100 activities are not sufficient to cover the *Catechism* in a comprehensive way. However, this book includes the major points of belief, such as the sacraments and commandments, as well as aspects of the faith that might not be fully addressed in basic catechism texts, such as prayer and Scripture.

It is hoped that these activities will enhance any Catholic religious education program and inspire the faith of students and teachers alike.

E. R.

"I Believe in One God, the Father . . ."

NAME _____

Write the names of some things God has created.

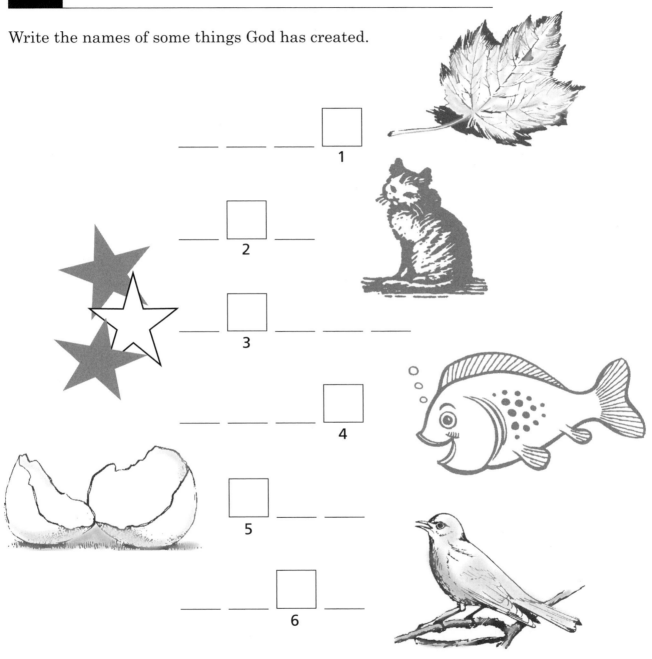

Use the letters from the numbered boxes above to finish this sentence.

God is our ☐ ☐ ☐ ☐ ☐ ☐.
1 2 3 4 5 6

Our Father

NAME

_____

When the Apostles asked Jesus how to pray, the answer He gave them was the prayer we call the Our Father. By looking at this prayer, we can learn more about the character of the First Person of the Holy Trinity, God the Father. Fill in each blank with the best word from the list below.

God's children Heaven needs hears merciful good grace strength greater holy

By praying this . . .

1. Our Father

2. Who art in Heaven

3. Hallowed be Thy Name

4. Thy Kingdom come

5. Thy will be done on earth as it is in Heaven

6. Give us this day our daily bread

7. And forgive us our trespasses

8. As we forgive those who trespass against us

9. And lead us not into temptation

10. But deliver us from evil

We can know this . . .

1. We are _____ of God.

2. To be with God means to be in _____.

3. God is _____.

4. We want _____ Kingdom of goodness, peace, and joy to spread to all people.

5. God wills only what is _____.

6. God provides for our _____.

7. God is _____.

8. With God's _____, we can and must show love and mercy to others.

9. God gives us free will, but He _____ us when we ask for help to avoid sin, and He gives us _____.

10. God is _____ than the devil.

3

"I Believe in One Lord Jesus Christ"

NAME _____

Use the words on the right to complete the sentences.

Jesus is the _____ of God.

He came down from _____.

_____ is Jesus' birthday.

Jesus has a human Mother.

Her name is _____.

God gave Jesus a _____ father.

His name is Joseph.

Jesus came to _____ all people

from their sins.

Jesus came to bring God's _____.

Christmas

foster

love

Heaven

save

Mary

Son

Jesus, Our Savior

NAME

God sent His Son, Jesus, to us on earth so that we could someday come to be with God in Heaven, where we will be happy forever.

The sentences below outline the story of our salvation. Number them in correct **time** order.

☐ Jesus stayed with His disciples for forty days, then ascended to His Father in Heaven.

☐ God created Adam and Eve in His own image.

☐ Jesus grew up in the town of Nazareth, where He studied, worked, and played; He was loved and cared for by Mary and Joseph, His Mother and foster-father, and He obeyed them.

☐ Jesus was baptized in the Jordan River by His cousin, John the Baptist; for the next three years He healed people, forgave their sins, and taught them about the love of His Father.

☐ Adam and Eve disobeyed God and had to leave the Garden of Eden.

☐ Mary said yes, she would become the Mother of Jesus.

☐ God sent many prophets and leaders to prepare the world for His Son.

☐ The Holy Spirit descended upon Jesus' followers on the day of Pentecost, which is known as the birthday of the Church.

☐ Jesus was crucified, died, and was buried; on the third day He rose from the dead.

The Name of Jesus

NAME

Use the following number code to complete the sentence beneath it.

A	B	C	D	E	F	G	H	I	J	K	L	M
1	2	3	4	5	6	7	8	9	10	11	12	13

N	O	P	Q	R	S	T	U	V	W	X	Y	Z
14	15	16	17	18	19	20	21	22	23	24	25	26

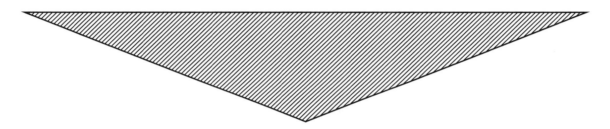

The name "Jesus" in Hebrew means

"__ __ __   __ __ __ __ __".
　7　15　4　　19　1　22　5　19

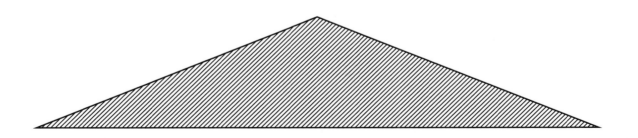

"He Suffered Death and Was Buried"

Circle these hidden words in the box below.

cross	died	Mary
Jesus	tomb	Good Friday
Pilate	soldiers	buried

```
F  B  X  M  G  L  D  I  S
G  J  C  R  O  S  S  M  L
C  E  M  T  O  M  B  U  F
J  S  A  L  D  I  E  D  A
E  U  R  A  F  R  B  Y  P
S  S  Y  M  R  M  U  L  D
S  O  L  D  I  E  R  S  N
R  T  O  S  D  I  I  D  L
Q  P  I  L  A  T  E  B  U
L  G  Y  S  Y  F  D  X  H
```

PRAY

Jesus, thank You for dying on the Cross to make up for my sins.

Amen.

100 Activities Based on the Catechism of the Catholic Church
© 2013 Ignatius Press

"And Rose Again on the Third Day"

NAME _____

Listen to your teacher read about Jesus' Resurrection from the Gospel of Matthew, chapter 28, verses 1 to 10. Then write the correct word to complete the following sentences.

Mary Magdalene and _____ came to the tomb.
(Peter / the other Mary)

The _____ said Jesus had been raised!
(guards / angel)

The women were very _____.
(happy / sad)

When they left to tell the disciples, they met _____.
(the angel / Jesus)

They _____ his feet.
(embraced / washed)

The angel and Jesus said the same words to the women.

Write the missing letters in this message.

"D_ n_t be _fr_id."

"I Believe in the Holy Spirit"

NAME _____

Read the story. Color the pictures.

When we pray, we make the Sign of the ✝. We say, "In the name of the Father, and of the Son, and of the Holy Spirit." Who is the Holy Spirit? We cannot 👁👁 Him. When Jesus was baptized, the Holy Spirit came down like a 🕊. After Jesus rose from the dead, the Holy Spirit came to Mary and the Apostles as 🔥. The Holy Spirit is with us today in the ⛪. We believe in the Holy Spirit.

. . . .

Color in the letters.

The Holy Spirit

TEACHER-DIRECTED ACTIVITY

Materials: drawing paper, drawing materials.

Directions

Say: Have you ever read a mystery book or seen a detective movie? In such a story a crime occurs, and it is up to police detectives or other investigators to figure out what happened and who was responsible. They didn't witness the event, but through the use of evidence—physical objects, statements from people, etc.—they solve the mystery.

God is a mystery—the most wonderful mystery we can imagine! We cannot fully understand God. We cannot see Him, but like a detective we believe in God because of the evidence He leaves. God the Father is evident in the world, in everything He created. God the Son became evident in the person of Jesus Christ, true God and true man.

What about the Third Person of the Trinity, the Holy Spirit? What clues does He leave?

Write the following on the board and discuss one at a time.

> We find the Holy Spirit in:
>
> > the Scriptures,
> >
> > the teaching of the Church through the popes and bishops,
> >
> > the Mass,
> >
> > prayer,
> >
> > the priesthood and other gifted service to the Church,
> >
> > missionaries who bring the good news of Jesus to all the world,
> >
> > and in the saints.

Pass out drawing materials, and ask students to draw an example of one of these. Post the drawings in the classroom.

The Church: The People of God

TEACHER-DIRECTED ACTIVITY

Say: The Church is the People of God. God does not belong to us; rather, we belong to him, through Baptism.

The word "church" comes from the Latin word *ecclesia*, which means a calling together, an assembly. Who makes up this assembly that is the Church? The Church includes the invisible, such as the saints in Heaven, and also the visible, the baptized Christians who live in this world. Today we will focus on the visible Church.

Directions

On the board, write out the six mystery words as shown below, with a line for each letter and one or more letters filled in for a clue. Read the sentences aloud and let the students figure out the correct words.

1.   **P** __ __ **E**

This is the title given to the head of the Church and the bishop of Rome. The first one to hold this office was Saint Peter the Apostle.

2.   **B** **I** __ __ __ **P** __

These are the leaders of the Church who follow after the Apostles. They are in charge of many parishes in a large area called a diocese. They are chosen by the person named in question 1.

3.   __ **R** **I** **E** __ **T** __

These assist the people named in number 2. They usually serve in parishes, where they preach and teach. They can say Mass, hear confessions, and give the Sacrament of the Sick. The people in questions 1 and 2 are also these.

4.   __ **E** **A** __ __ **N**

Some men are ordained to serve the Church but do not say Mass or hear confessions. They can baptize and officiate at a marriage; they can participate in the Mass through proclaiming the Gospel, giving the homily, and also serving the People of God in many ways outside the liturgy.

5.   **H** __ **L** __

The laity are the People of God who are not ordained: This includes you and me! Our role is to bring the good news about Jesus to those around us by doing our daily responsibilities. Like all the people named in the first four answers, we are called to be _____.

6.   **M** **A** __ __ __

There are people who are laity, because they are not ordained, yet they set themselves apart for the service of God and the Church. Some live in a religious community as sisters or brothers. They take vows of poverty, chastity, and obedience, and therefore they do not _____.

Note: As an alternative, you could also lead this activity like a "hangman" game, but instead of drawing parts of the hangman figure for each incorrect letter guessed, you can draw parts of a simple church—the walls, doors, steeple, etc.—for each correct letter.

Your Baptism

NAME

When you were baptized, you received God's life of grace. You joined the family of God. Circle the things that were part of your Baptism celebration. Color the pictures.

The Sacrament of Baptism

NAME

Circle the correct answer.

Baptism takes away sin.
Yes   No

A person can be baptized only once.
Yes   No

Only babies are baptized.
Yes   No

Baptism gives us the Holy Spirit.
Yes   No

The Mass

NAME

Help Father get ready for Mass. Circle the things he will need.
Cross out the things he will not need.

The Mass and Our Senses

God did not make us pure spirits like the angels. He gave us bodies too. When we worship at Mass, we use all our senses to experience the love of God.

After looking at the pictures, write the number on the lines for things we receive through our senses at Mass. (Most will have more than one answer.)

I see: _____

I hear: _____

I touch: _____

I taste: _____

I smell: _____

1. Incense

2. Holy Communion

3. Reading of the Gospel

4. The Sign of Peace

5. The Altar

6. Candle

7. The Crucifix

8. Singing

Preparing to Receive Holy Communion

NAME _____

Choose the correct word or words to complete the sentences.

Before we receive Holy Communion, we must be free from all serious sins;

another name for a serious sin is _____ sin. We can receive God's
mortal / venial

forgiveness for serious sins through the Sacrament of _____.
Confirmation / Reconciliation

Also before we receive Communion, the Church asks that we fast for at least

_____. To fast means to go without _____ out of
one hour / one night   sweets / food

reverence for the Body of our Lord, which we are about to receive. The

Church encourages her people to receive _____ each
Communion / Reconciliation

time they go to Mass. During the first part of the Mass, called the Liturgy of

the _____, we can listen and pray, so that we will be ready
Eucharist / Word

to receive Jesus' Body and Blood. We can ask for faith to believe that during

the _____ the bread and wine are really
Lord's Prayer / Eucharistic Prayer

changed into the Body and Blood of Christ. When it is our turn to receive

Communion, the priest or special minister of the Eucharist says, "The Body

of Christ". We answer, _____, to say, "Yes, I believe
"Amen" / "Alleluia"

this is Jesus Himself."

Receiving Holy Communion: A Practice Session

TEACHER-DIRECTED ACTIVITY

Materials: unconsecrated communion hosts (one per student), paten or small bowl.

Purpose: to prepare to receive First Holy Communion.

Note: Make prior arrangements to use the church or a chapel for this practice. If possible, meet first in your regular classroom, then proceed as a class to the church. Adjust these directions to local practice, location of tabernacle, and so forth.

Directions

In the classroom, explain to the students that you will be taking them to the church (or chapel) to rehearse their First Communion.

Ask: What does it mean to rehearse something? [*Practice.*]

Is a rehearsal the same as the event itself? Is a dance practice the same as the performance? [*No.*]

Say: That's right. When a man and woman plan to marry, they hold a rehearsal so they can remember what to do and say at their wedding. They aren't married until the actual wedding, when they say their promises, or vows, to each other.

We're going to do something similar today. It's very easy to receive Communion, but sometimes people get a little nervous or distracted by all the excitement of their First Communion. This practice will help you to remember what to do and say. Even with all the attention and special clothes and flowers and pictures, the only really important thing about your First Communion is Jesus and you—Jesus loving you, and you receiving Him and loving Him in return.

Since a practice is not the actual sacrament, we will not be giving you the Body of Christ today. I will pretend to be the priest or

special minister of the Eucharist, and what I will give you is an unconsecrated host. Has anyone heard the term "unconsecrated host"? [*It is a host that has not been changed into the Body of Jesus by the priest at Mass.*]

Yes, it means the little wafer of bread that looks like bread, smells like bread, tastes like bread, and really is bread, only bread. When you receive Jesus in the Eucharist, the Host looks like bread, smells like bread, and tastes like bread, but isn't bread at all any more—the wafer has been changed into the Body and Blood, Soul and Divinity of our Lord! Our minds cannot understand it, but our minds believe it.

So, I will say the words, "The Body of Christ" (even though we know this time it isn't), and you will answer, "Amen". You will hold your hands out like a beggar, your right hand cupping your left. I will place the unconsecrated host in your left hand. While facing the altar, you will pick it up with your right hand, put it in your mouth, and eat it. [*Demonstrate this as you speak.*] You will then fold your hands and walk slowly to your pew (or seat), kneel, and say a silent prayer.

Note: If local practice calls for receiving Communion on the tongue or from the chalice, instruct students accordingly.

Say: The time of prayer after Communion is a very special time. You and Jesus are as close as you can be! You can talk to Him about anything. You can listen to Him speak to you in your thoughts. You can praise Him for His goodness and love. You can thank Him for being your Friend and your Savior. You can ask Him to help or heal family and friends. You can seek His help in being a better follower of His. I will lead you in a sample prayer today when all of you have come back to your seats.

Continued

Receiving Holy Communion: A Practice Session

Remember, when we enter the church today, that, even though Jesus is not the host I'll be giving you, He is present as consecrated Hosts in the tabernacle. So we honor Him by genuflecting toward the tabernacle before we sit down or kneel. How do we genuflect? Can someone demonstrate? [*Call on one child.*]

That's right, we touch the right knee to the floor. So, go right up to the first pews (rows), genuflect, move all the way down, and be seated silently. Any questions before we go? Let's line up!

In the church, you might conduct a brief review of the parts of the Mass. Then, proceed through the practice as you explained to the students. After all have received the practice host, have them repeat after you the lines of this prayer:

Thank You, Jesus, for preparing me to receive You for the first time.

Thank You for my parents, my teachers, and the priest(s) of our church.

I am so happy that I will soon be so close to You.

You are great and holy.

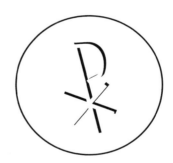

I love You.

Help me as I grow up so I can be more like You. Amen.

Proceed back to classroom, all genuflecting as they leave and blessing themselves with holy water as a reminder of Baptism.

Additional Activity

Distribute copies of Activity 23, "My Prayer". Ask the students to compose their own prayer to say after receiving Jesus for the first time. They may write it in class or take it home for homework.

The Holy Trinity

TEACHER-DIRECTED ACTIVITY

Directions

On the board, draw the figure and write out the words to the song. Pass out pieces of paper and crayons or markers.

Say:

The most important belief we hold as Christians is that God is a Holy Trinity. This means that there are three persons in one God: The Father, the Son and the Holy Spirit. None of the persons is greater than the other. Each is fully God, immortal, and equal in majesty and power.

There are many beautiful hymns about the Holy Trinity. Here is a simple song that can help us think about the mystery of the Holy Trinity. (Lead the class in singing this song to the tune of "Twinkle, Twinkle Little Star".)

> *Father, Son and Spirit three,*
> *You are the Holy Trinity;*
>
> *In Three Persons, One God who*
> *Is holy, mighty, immortal too;*
>
> *Three in one divinity—*
> *This is faith's great mystery.*

Say: Three persons, one God. How can this be? Even the saints could not fully understand this great mystery, a truth that can only be known by faith. Although we may not be able to explain it, we can describe the Trinity with images.

Saint Patrick of Ireland used the image of the single **clover**, which has three leaves.

Others have used the image of **water**, which can be in the form of water, ice, or steam, but remains water.

Some have compared the Holy Trinity to **fire**, which is one element with three different purposes: It cooks food, heats a room, and gives light.

Another way to think about the Holy Trinity is to think of a **person**. A man can be a son, a brother, and a father. A woman can be a sister, mother, daughter. They are one person, but differ in their relationships to others.

We can think of the Trinity as a **family** and see that our own families are modeled on God as a "communion of persons". Like the Father, parents share in creation by giving life to children; like the Son, the family shares in the sacrifice of Christ through Mass, prayer and holy living; and like the Spirit, the family can bring the Word of God to others.

Now, draw a picture of the Holy Trinity using one of the images described above, or your own idea. Know that no picture will be perfect—this is, after all, the greatest mystery of our faith!

We Follow Jesus

 NAME

Jesus always did what God the Father wanted Him to do. If we follow Jesus, we will also please God and be happy. Match an action you can do with the example Jesus set for us in His earthly life. Connect the dots to match the actions.

WHAT WE CAN DO

Put away my toys. •

Visit a relative in the hospital. •

Play with a younger brother or sister. •

Talk to God during the day. •

Put some money in the collection • for the poor.

Invite a friend to Mass. •

Play with someone who seems lonely. •

WHAT JESUS DID

• *Loved children.*

• *Prayed.*

• *Obeyed His mother and foster father.*

• *Gave people food.*

• *Told people about God's love.*

• *Helped the sick.*

• *Loved people whom others did not like.*

We Love God

NAME _____

God gave us the Ten Commandments as His laws of love. The first three tell us how to love God. Write the number of the Commandment next to the sentences that tell ways you can follow that Commandment.

1. You shall not have other gods besides Me.

2. You shall not use God's name in vain.

3. Remember to keep God's day holy.

_____ 1. You go to Mass each Sunday and holy day.

_____ 2. You look up to Jesus more than to sports or movie stars.

_____ 3. You use God's name when you pray to Him.

_____ 4. You talk about God with respect.

_____ 5. You trust God alone to give you what you need.

_____ 6. You spend some time on Sundays looking at the Bible or other religious books.

PRAY

God, my Father, Your Commandments will help me to be happy with You now and in Heaven. Thank You for Your laws of love.

100 Activities Based on the Catechism of the Catholic Church
© 2013 Ignatius Press

We Love Our Neighbor

NAME

The last seven Commandments tell us how to love our neighbor.
Write the number of the Commandment next to the sentence that
tells one way to follow it.

4. Honor your father and your mother.

5. You shall not kill.

6. You shall not commit adultery.

7. You shall not steal.

8. You shall not lie.

9. You shall not covet your neighbor's wife.

10. You shall not covet your neighbor's goods.

_____ 1. You tell your teacher the real reason for being late.

_____ 2. When you are mad at your brother, you cool off instead of hitting
him.

_____ 3. You thank God for the good things He gives you.

_____ 4. You obey your parents.

_____ 5. You ask your dad for the quarter on his dresser before you take it.

_____ 6. You treat your body with modesty and respect.

_____ 7. You are thankful for your own family.

_____ 8. You do your chores cheerfully.

_____ 9. You avoid untrue talk about others.

The Beatitudes

NAME _____

Along with your teacher, read the Gospel of Matthew, chapter 5, verses 1 to 12, from the Bible. Then match each action or attitude in the Beatitudes with God's promise for each one.

1. ____ The poor in spirit . . .

2. ____ Those who mourn . . .

3. ____ The meek . . .

4. ____ Those who hunger and thirst for righteousness . . .

5. ____ The merciful . . .

6. ____ The pure in heart . . .

7. ____ The peacemakers . . .

8. ____ Those who are persecuted for righteousness' sake . . .

A. shall obtain mercy.

B. shall be comforted.

C. theirs is the Kingdom of Heaven.

D. shall inherit the earth.

E. shall be satisfied.

F. shall see God.

G. shall be called sons of God.

H. theirs is the Kingdom of Heaven.

The Holy Family and My Family

NAME

Human society begins with a family. The first human beings, Adam and Eve, were formed by God to be a family and are called our "first parents". You and everyone living were born into a family, and your family is your own first society.

God could have come into the world any way he wished. He chose to come into a family. Jesus, Mary, and Joseph are the Holy Family. We pray to be like them.

Read the phrases below. If a phrase is true about your family, circle the picture of the HOUSE. If it is true about the Holy Family, circle the image of the HOLY FAMILY. If a phrase is true for both, circle both images.

1. Follows the Ten Commandments

2. Drives to church

3. Flees to another country to protect a child's life

4. Worships God as a family

5. Loses a child and then finds him

6. Parents teach in words and actions about God

7. Watches television or movies together

8. Parents provide for and protect the family

My Prayer

TEACHER-DIRECTED ACTIVITY

Note: This activity could accompany Activity 16, "Receiving Holy Communion: A Practice Session", or be used as a separate activity.

Directions

Say: Saint John Damascene teaches us that "prayer is the raising of one's mind and heart to God." There are five basic forms of prayer.

Write the name of each form of prayer on the board as you say:

1. ***Blessing and adoration***
   We bless God or call Him blessed because of His love and goodness; we adore Him, that is, we give Him heartfelt love and worship because He is our Creator.

2. ***Petition***
   We ask God for what we need, especially for forgiveness.

3. ***Intercession***
   We ask God to help others, even our enemies.

4. ***Thanksgiving***
   We thank God for all His gifts. Even in difficulty, we ask Him for the good He will bring out of it.

5. ***Praise***
   We give glory to God just because He is God, not for what He does, but for Who He is.

Now let's see if as a class we can think of a prayer using each of these forms.

Go down the list and call on students to give examples of each prayer form. Write the examples on the board as they are given. Then erase the prayers.

Pass out copies of the following page and say:

It's your turn to write a prayer of your own, using the forms of prayer you have learned. Simply finish the sentences with your own words.

MY PRAYER

Jesus, I love You because _____

_____

Please forgive all of my sins and help me _____

_____

Also, Jesus, please _____

_____

I pray for _____, who needs

_____

I thank You, Jesus, for _____

_____

I praise You for _____

_____

The First Form of Prayer: Blessing

NAME _____

God blesses us when he gives us good things. And when we receive these as gifts, we in turn bless God.

Here are some blessing prayers you may know. Underline the word "bless" in each prayer. Then draw a line to match each prayer with the correct picture.

A.

B.

C.

D.

1. Bless us, O Lord, and these Thy gifts, which we are about to receive from Thy bounty, through Christ our Lord.

2. Glory to God in the highest, and on earth peace to people of good will. We praise You, we bless You, we adore You, we glorify You, we give You thanks for Your great glory, Lord God, heavenly King, O God, almighty Father.

3. My dear friends, let us turn to the Lord and pray that He will bless with His grace this woman now married in Christ to this man, and that through the Sacrament of the Body and Blood of Christ He will unite in love the couple He has joined in this holy bond.

4. May God, who created the animals of this earth as a help to us, continue to protect and sustain us with the grace His blessing brings, now and for ever.

Jesus, I Adore You

NAME

At Mass, the priest changes the bread and wine on the altar into the Body and Blood of Jesus. After Mass, the Body of Christ that was not received by the people in Holy Communion is reserved in the tabernacle in the church. Often the tabernacle is behind the altar, but in some churches it is in a chapel or another special place. Wherever the tabernacle is located, a candle burns nearby to show us that Jesus is present. Throughout the day, we can enter a Catholic Church and visit Jesus there.

Sometimes the Blessed Sacrament is displayed in a monstrance, a beautiful container placed on the altar, for a time of special adoration.

The letters of the word ADORE are hidden in this picture of a monstrance.

Find the letters and trace them.

A Prayer for Divine Mercy

TEACHER-DIRECTED ACTIVITY

Activity A

Say:

Jesus gave up his life for us on Good Friday. At three o'clock in the afternoon, he died on the Cross; and when a soldier pierced his heart with a spear, blood and water poured out. His body was taken down and buried. Then on Easter Sunday, Jesus rose from the dead, showing us that his love is more powerful than death.

A holy nun from Poland, Saint Faustina Kowalska, taught that when Jesus died, he poured out his mercy like a fountain for the whole world. The Church celebrates this Divine Mercy as a feast day, designated by Pope John Paul II to be celebrated on the Sunday after Easter.

Every day we can remember the Divine Mercy by praying to Jesus at three o'clock, no matter where we are or what we are doing. This is a simple prayer from Saint Faustina that we can pray:

Jesus, I trust in You.

Let's say this prayer together.

(*Repeat with the class.*)

Activity B

Distribute copies of the next page to the class.

A Prayer for Divine Mercy

NAME

Complete the pattern above by tracing over the Cross and the words.
Draw a heart shape around the words.

Mary, Mother of Christ

NAME

The Church has given us this beautiful prayer to Mary, the
Mother of Jesus.

> Hail, Mary, full of grace.
> The Lord is with thee.
> Blessed art thou among women,
> and blessed is the fruit of thy womb, Jesus.
>
> Holy Mary, Mother of God,
> pray for us sinners
> now and at the hour of our death. Amen.

The first part of the prayer comes from the Bible. Listen to your
teacher read the Gospel of Luke, chapter 1, verses 26 to 45. Raise
your hand when you hear words from the Hail Mary prayer.

When God asked Mary to be the Mother of Jesus, she agreed.

Color in the X shapes in the pattern below for the word we
should say when God asks something of us.

Old and New Testaments

TEACHER-DIRECTED ACTIVITY

Activity A

Materials: Bibles, one per student and teacher.

Purpose: to begin to familiarize students with the Bible, its basic divisions, and the name of the books that comprise it.

Directions

Distribute the Bibles.

Say: Our Catholic Faith comes to us from two sources, the teaching we receive from our bishops and pope now and back through the ages to the original Apostles—what we call the apostolic Tradition—and Sacred Scripture, the Bible. Does anyone know what the word "Bible" means? [*"Book"—from the Greek language*]

Let's spend a few minutes with the Bible, getting to know it a little bit. Just open it up, anywhere, and read silently for a moment. [*Give students about five minutes for this exercise, longer if they remain focused.*]

Okay, let's share a little about what we read. [*Call on several students. Be open to what they may offer, even if they suggest they couldn't understand what they read—many adults feel intimidated by the Bible. Ask students if they saw any names they recognized, stories they had heard, prayers they know. Discuss.*]

The Bible contains stories, poems, songs, and prayers. For example, our most important Christian prayer comes from the Gospel of Matthew in the Bible. Can you tell me what it is? [*The Our Father—Mt 6:9–13*]

Also, the first half of the Hail Mary comes right out of the Gospel of Luke in the Bible (Lk 1:28, 42). When we go to Mass, we don't usually bring our Bibles with us. Is the Bible part of our Mass? [*Yes, the Liturgy of the Word—the first part of the Mass—includes readings from the Bible. We can follow along in the missalettes, which have the readings printed for each week.*]

Have your Bible marked at the beginning of the New Testament and at the table of contents noting the books in both the Old and New Testaments. Open up your Bible to where the New Testament begins, to demonstrate the two sections.

Say: The Bible is divided into two main sections. Do you know what they are called? [*The Old Testament and the New Testament*] The first section is the Old Testament, and it contains the story of creation, the history of the Israelites, the Psalms of David, and the prophets—the people God called to prepare the world for the coming of Jesus. Look at the first few pages of your Bibles and see if you can tell me how many books there are in the Old Testament. [*46*]

Now, let's race to find the beginning of the New Testament. When you find the listing of books in the New Testament, tell me how many there are. [*27*] The New Testament contains what? [*The Gospels, the letters of Saint Paul, Saint Peter, Saint John, and others.*] It tells the story of Jesus and the first Christians. Okay, close your Bibles for a minute. I am going to name a book, and I want you to turn to the Bible and tell us whether it is in the Old or the New Testament.

Note: You can go down the row, student by student, so everyone has a turn, or let everyone in class look up the books at the same time, and the first one to raise his hand is called on to give the answer. A third option is a relay race (see **Activity B**, next page). Choose books at random, or use the following list:

1. First Letter of John (NT)	11. First and Second Chronicles (OT)
2. Genesis (OT)	12. Jeremiah (OT)
3. First Kings (OT)	13. Colossians (NT)
4. Gospel of Mark (NT)	14. Jude (NT)
5. Isaiah (OT)	15. Job (OT)
6. Revelation (NT)	16. Habakkuk (OT)
7. Joel (OT)	17. Titus (NT)
8. Second Corinthians (NT)	18. Song of Solomon (OT)
9. Acts of the Apostles (NT)	19. Galatians (NT)
10. Ruth (OT)	20. Numbers (OT)

Old and New Testaments

TEACHER-DIRECTED ACTIVITY

Activity B

Materials: Bibles, paper, pencils.

Directions

Using the list of Bible books (book names only) from **Activity A**, copy ten names per sheet, onto two sheets of paper.

Divide the class into two teams. Give the first player on each team a Bible, one of the lists, and a pencil. The players on each team are to take turns, and the teams are race to be the first to finish writing "O" (for Old Testament) or "N" (for New Testament) next to the names of each book in the list. They may use the table of contents in their Bible if needed.

After the first team player has finished, he passes the Bible, the list, and the pencil to the next player, who identifies the next name on the list. The list passes through the team, like a baton in a relay race, until all of the books have been designated "O" or "N". The first team to finish the list correctly wins.

100 Activities Based on the Catechism of the Catholic Church
© 2013 Ignatius Press

Find That Verse

TEACHER-DIRECTED ACTIVITY

Materials: Bibles.

Directions

Divide the class into two or more equal teams, giving a Bible to the first player in each.

Call out the first citation from the list at the right to the class. The competing players race to find it in the Bible, and when they do they raise their hands. The first to raise his hand is called upon to read the citation aloud. If correct, he earns a point for his team.

The Bibles are then passed to the next players on each team. The game continues in the same fashion until all of the team members have had a turn.

The team with the most points is the winner.

1. 1 John 5:3
2. Genesis 1:27
3. 1 Kings 2:11
4. Mark 12:30
5. Isaiah 12:2
6. Revelation 4:8
7. Joel 2:15
8. 2 Corinthians 13:14
9. Acts 12:1
10. Ruth 1:16
11. 1 Chronicles 16:34
12. Jeremiah 51:15
13. Colossians 3:20
14. Jude 2
15. Job 1:1
16. Habakkuk 3:19
17. Titus 2:11
18. Song of Solomon 2:1
19. Galatians 3:27
20. Numbers 15:40

Abbreviations for Books of the Bible

NAME _____

In written English we use many kinds of abbreviations. For example, we write **Mr.** instead of spelling out **Mister**. We have abbreviations for the names of the books of the Bible. See if you can match some of the names with the abbreviations below.

1. ____ 1 Mac		**A.**	Genesis
2. ____ Acts		**B.**	Psalms
3. ____ 2 Pet		**C.**	Song of Solomon
4. ____ Jas		**D**	Isaiah
5. ____ Eph		**E.**	1 Maccabees
6. ____ 3 Jn		**F.**	Matthew
7. ____ Gen		**G.**	Acts of the Apostles
8. ____ Rev		**H.**	Ephesians
9. ____ Is		**I.**	2 Peter
10. ____ Mt		**J.**	James
11. ____ Song		**K.**	3 John
12. ____ Ps		**L.**	Revelation

The People of the Gospels

TEACHER-DIRECTED ACTIVITY

Materials: index cards prepared with names and Scripture references, tape, Bibles, paper, three token prizes (e.g., rosary, holy card).

Purpose: to deepen students' knowledge of the people who were touched by Christ.

GAME

Directions

Using the list given below, write one name and its Scripture notation on one side of each index card. Do not show the names to the students.

Say: Today we are going to play a game similar to a party game you may have played before. It's similar to Twenty Questions also. Please listen carefully to the directions. I am going to tape to each of your backs an index card with the name of a person from the Gospels. This is your secret identity. The object of the game is to be the first one to guess your identity.

Here's how you play: You mingle around the room and find another student to talk to. You may ask him three questions about yourself that can be answered "Yes" or "No". For example, "Am I a man?" "Am I a disciple?" "Does Jesus heal me?" That student can then ask three questions about his identity. (You look at each other's cards, of course, but not your own.) After three questions, you move on to another student and ask three more questions. You continue like this until you correctly guess who you are.

Note: Depending on how well prepared your students are, you may want to give them a few minutes with their Bibles to read the Gospel verses to refresh their memories about some of the people.

Say: Here are a few hints: These are real people, not characters from the parables that Jesus told. Not every person in the Gospels is known by a name. For example, the Samaritan woman at the well, the one to whom Jesus offered living water, is never referred to by her name but, rather, as "the woman at the well". Also, you might be more than one person, for example, the soldiers who ar-

rested Jesus. Stretch your memories and your imagination! As soon as you've guessed correctly, come up to me—the first three will get a little prize. Save your cards for the next activity.

People to choose from:

1. Elizabeth, mother of John—Luke 1:39–45
2. Mary, Mother of Jesus—Luke 1:26–38
3. Joseph, husband of Mary—Matthew 2:13–15
4. John the Baptist—Mark 1:2–11
5. Three Wise Men—Matthew 2:1–12
6. King Herod—Luke 23:6–12
7. Peter—Luke 5:1–11
8. Andrew—Matthew 4:18–20
9. James—Mark 10:35–45
10. John, the Apostle—John 19:25–27 (*refers to himself as "the disciple whom Jesus loved"*)
11. Thomas—John 20:24–29
12. Judas Iscariot—Matthew 26:14–16, 20–25
13. A leper—Matthew 8:1–4
14. The faithful centurion—Matthew 8:5–13
15. The paralyzed man—Mark 2:1–12
16. Jairus' daughter—Mark 5:21–24, 35–43
17. Simeon—Luke 2:25–32
18. Rich young man—Matthew 19:16–22
19. Boy with a demon—Matthew 17:14–18
20. Children—Matthew 19:13–15
21. Nicodemus—John 3:1–15
22. Blind beggar—Luke 18:35–43
23. Pharisees—Matthew 23:1–12
24. Lazarus—John 11:38–44
25. Mary, Lazarus' sister—Luke 10:38–42
26. Martha, Lazarus' sister—John 11:17–27
27. Zacchaeus—Luke 19:1–10
28. Pontius Pilate—John 18:28–40, 19:1–16
29. Mary Magdalene—John 20:11–18
30. The good thief—Luke 23:39–43
31. The woman who dried the Lord's feet with her hair—Luke 7:36–50

WORKSHEET

Give each student an "identity card", as above, and a copy of the Activity 32 worksheet. Each student needs also a Bible and pencil or pen.

32

Encountering Jesus

NAME _____

Your teacher will give you the name of a person mentioned in the
Gospels and the notation for the passage in which the person is
mentioned. Read the passage in the Bible.

Put yourself in the place of the person and think about what it was
like to have had a personal encounter with Jesus. Use your
imagination to place yourself in the Gospel passage and think about
how Jesus affected you. Then answer the following questions.

1. Who am I?

2. What happened between Jesus and me?

3. What are my feelings about this experience?

4. What will I do now?

Our Forefathers in Faith

NAME _____

"Now faith is the assurance of what is hoped for and the conviction of things not seen." So begins Chapter 11 of the Letter to the Hebrews in the New Testament. The author of the letter goes on to praise several of the Old Testament fathers of faith, who clung fast to the promises of God even though they did not live to see them fulfilled. This litany of faith encourages us to follow the example of the ancient believers and be hopeful in times of trial.

Read the entire chapter in the Bible, then match the name on the left to the description on the right.

____ 1. Abel

____ 2. Enoch

____ 3. Noah

____ 4. Abraham

____ 5. Isaac

____ 6. Jacob

____ 7. Joseph

____ 8. Moses

____ 9. Rahab

A. Housed two spies sent by Joshua, and so was spared at the fall of Jericho

B. A predecessor of Noah, he was taken up to heaven before his death, a sign of his favor with God

C. Called by God to leave his homeland; though childless, he was promised many descendants

D. Son of Abraham, he also heard God's voice and believed in the promise of a great nation

E. A keeper of flocks who gave God his best lamb as an offering

F. Commanded by God to be fertile and multiply; God sent a rainbow as a sign of his covenant with him

G. Given the name "Israel" after his struggle with an angel; he fathered twelve sons and lived to bless his grandsons

H. Escaped from Egypt, then returned to lead God's people toward the promised land

I. Was betrayed by his brothers and sold into slavery, but came to greatness in Egypt.

The Apostles' Creed

NAME _____

The word "creed" comes from the Latin word *credo*, which means "I believe". The Apostles' Creed is a summary, or short version, of the beliefs of Jesus' first chosen followers. The Apostles' Creed is most commonly recited at the beginning of the Rosary, and it is a good one to memorize. When we say the Creed and believe the words we say, we draw close to God. Saint Ambrose called the Creed "the treasure of our soul".

Using the clues below each line, fill in the blanks to complete the Apostles' Creed.

(1) I believe in God, the _____ almighty, Creator of
　　　　　　　　　　　　　　　(First Person of the Blessed Trinity)

_____ and earth, (2) and in Jesus Christ, his only _____,
　(our true home)　　　　　　　　　　　　　　　　　　　　　　　　(male child)

our Lord, (3) who was conceived by the _____, born of
　　　　　　　　　　　　　　　　　　　(Third Person of the Trinity)

the Virgin _____, (4) suffered under Pontius Pilate, was
　　　　　(Jesus' Mother)

_____, died and was buried. (5) He descended into hell; (6) on the
(executed on a cross)

_____ day he rose again from the dead; (7) he ascended into heaven,
(between second and fourth)

and is seated at the _____ hand of God the Father almighty; (8) from there
　　　　　　　　　　(opposite of left)

he will come again to judge the living and the _____. (9) I _____
　　　　　　　　　　　　　　　　　　　　　　　(not living)　　　　　(put faith in)

in the Holy Spirit, the holy catholic _____, the communion of
　　　　　　　　　　　　　　　　　　(people of God)

_____, (10) the forgiveness of _____, the resurrection of the
　(holy people)　　　　　　　　　　　　　　　(moral wrongs)

body, and _____ everlasting. Amen.
　　　　(opposite of death)

The Nicene Creed

At each Sunday Mass, after the priest gives a homily, we stand together and profess our Faith, that is, recite a summary of the most important beliefs we share as members of the Church. The profession of faith we make is usually the Nicene Creed. This Creed ("creed" comes from the Latin word *credo*, or "I believe") was composed as a result of two great councils of bishops, held in the cities of Nicaea and Constantinople in the fourth century. Think of it: With only minor changes in the translation from the original Greek, for seventeen centuries Catholics across the globe have professed the same summary of our Faith!

Read over the Nicene Creed, below. Then answer the questions on the activity sheet.

• •

1. I believe in one God,
    the Father almighty,
    maker of heaven and earth,
    of all things visible and invisible.

2. I believe in one Lord, Jesus Christ,
    the Only Begotten Son of God,
    born of the Father before all ages.
    God from God, Light from Light,
    true God from true God,
    begotten, not made,
    consubstantial with the Father;
  through him all things were made.

3. For us men and for our salvation
    he came down from heaven,
  and by the Holy Spirit
    was incarnate of the Virgin Mary,
    and became man.

4. For our sake he was crucified under
    Pontius Pilate,
  he suffered death and was buried,

5. and rose again on the third day
    in accordance with the Scriptures.
  He ascended into heaven
    and is seated at the right hand
    of the Father.

6. He will come again in glory to judge
    the living and the dead,
    and his kingdom will have no end.

7. I believe in the Holy Spirit,
    the Lord, the giver of life,
    who proceeds from the Father
      and the Son,
  who with the Father and the Son
    is adored and glorified,
  who has spoken through the Prophets.

8. I believe in one, holy, catholic,
    and apostolic Church.

9. I confess one Baptism
    for the forgiveness of sins

10. and I look forward to
    the resurrection of the dead
      and the life of the world to come.
      Amen.

The Nicene Creed

NAME
_____

Refer to the words of the Nicene Creed to answer the questions. After each question is the section of the Creed where the answer can be found.

1. What personal name do we use when we talk about, or to, the almighty God, Creator of everything? (1)

   _____

2. The Son of God was not created by God, as Adam was. In a way that is beyond our human understanding, he comes from the Father while always existing with the Father. What word in the Creed expresses this mystery? (2)

   _____

3. Why did the Son of God become man? (3)

   _____

   _____

4. What was the name of the Roman ruler who permitted the crucifixion of Jesus Christ? (4)

   _____

5. What three things did Jesus willingly undergo "for our sake"? (4)

   _____

   _____

6. Jesus' coming, his death, and his Resurrection were not an accident, but part of God's eternal plan. What do we call the writings in which this plan of salvation is revealed? (5)

   _____

7. Where is Christ now? (5)

   _____

8. The first time the Son of God came to earth it was in humility; only those with faith recognized him. When he comes a second and final time, all will recognize him, and his authority will be complete. How will he come? (6)

   _____

9. The Holy Spirit comes from the Father and the Son, yet is just as fully God; the Three Persons are One. What sentence in the Creed expresses this equality? (7)

   _____

10. Through whom has the Holy Spirit spoken? (7)

    _____

11. What are the four characteristics, or marks, of Christ's Church? (8)

    _____

    _____

    _____

    _____

12. What is the primary sacrament for the forgiveness of sins? (9)

    _____

13. The Christian need not fear his own death nor the end of the world as we know it. What two things do we hope for? (10)

    _____

Memorizing the Creeds

TEACHER-DIRECTED ACTIVITY

Materials: copies of either Activity 34 (the Apostles' Creed) or Activity 35 (the Nicene Creed).

Purpose: to guide students in memorizing the Creeds.

Directions

Instruct the students to count off, 1 through 10, repeating the number series as needed so that every student has a number. Give the students a minute to read over the entire Creed silently, and then to concentrate on the statement that corresponds to their assigned number.

Beginning with the "Number 1" students and ending with "Number 10", have the students stand and recite their statement. For example, the "Number 1s" would stand and say, "I believe in one God, the Father almighty, maker of heaven and earth." They may sit or remain standing, and then the "Number 2s" would stand and recite "I believe in one Lord Jesus Christ, the Only Begotten Son of God."

After one round, have the students turn their papers over and give their statement from memory. Once this is done successfully, you may group some of the numbers together. For example, the 1s and 2s would give the first two statements together; the 3s and 4s recite the third and fourth together; and so on. After that, you could divide them into 1 through 5 and 6 through 10. After this, or in another class period, you can have the students say the entire Creed together from memory.

Spontaneous recitations through the year can reinforce this lesson, as can the praying of the Rosary at home and in class on feast days and other occasions.

The Attributes of God

NAME _____

Using a dictionary and the Bible, write the definition of each of the attributes of God listed below, and then write the Scripture passage that describes each attribute. (An attribute is a characteristic or trait of a person.)

1. **Omnipotent** _____
   Matthew 19:26 _____

2. **Omniscient** _____
   Psalm 139:1–2 _____

3. **Sovereign** _____
   Isaiah 46:9–10 _____

4. **Holy** _____
   Luke 1:49 _____

5. **Just** _____
   Isaiah 5:16 _____

6. **Everlasting** _____
   Exodus 15:18 _____

7. **Wise** _____
   Proverbs 3:19 _____

8. **Faithful** _____
   1 John 1:9 _____

9. **Good** _____
   John 10:11 _____

God Is Our Perfect Father

NAME

God, our heavenly Father, is perfect: he is all-powerful, all-knowing, and all-good. He made us out of love. One way we can learn about God and his love is through the teaching and example of our human father and mother. Our parents are not perfect, as God is; but they love us, and they try to do what is right.

The sentences below describe the actions of parents. For each sentence, write in an attribute of God the Father that the action can reflect. (An attribute is a characteristic or quality of a person or thing.)

ATTRIBUTES OF GOD THE FATHER

**life-giving
just
holy
merciful
kind
wise
generous**

_____ 1. Parents work hard to give their families food, clothing, and shelter.

_____ 2. Parents take special care of their children when they are sick.

_____ 3. Parents give much of their time and attention to their children.

_____ 4. Parents try to do what is right by obeying laws and paying taxes.

_____ 5. Fathers and mothers, joined together with God, bring children into the world.

_____ 6. Parents know and can teach us many things about God and his world.

_____ 7. Parents comfort their children when they are hurt or afraid.

_____ 8. Parents make rules for their children so that they will do what is right.

_____ 9. Parents forgive us when we have done something wrong.

_____ 10. Parents pray and try to follow Jesus' example.

The Story of Creation

NAME _____

Read the first chapter of the Book of Genesis. Then complete the
exercise below by filling in the missing words.

1. The first chapter in Genesis tells us many important truths about God, our Creator.
   From it we learn that God made the world and all living things out of nothing, just
   by willing them to be. "Then God said, 'Let there be light,' and there was light"
   (Gen 1:3). God is omnipotent, or all-_____.

2. We can look at the world around us and see how interesting and beautiful it is.
   Several verses in this chapter tell us that God himself was pleased with what he
   made: "God saw how good it was." A bad musician cannot make good music. A bad
   cook cannot make a good meal. So we can know that, if all creation is good, God, its
   Maker, is all-_____.

3. The chapter we read describes in detail which things God created on each day of the
   week. From this we learn that God did not just throw the world together. He has an
   order, a plan, and design, for his creation. God is omniscient, or all-_____.

4. Genesis reminds us of some very important things about us, too. God did not create
   just one kind of person, but rather, two, which we call _____ and
   _____. Also, God created people to be like himself, not in all ways,
   but in some special ways. We are made in God's _____.

The Days of Creation

NAME

Read the first chapter of the Book of Genesis. Then match the created thing with the creation day by drawing a connecting line or arrow.

The Angels

NAME _____

True or False

Circle the correct answer for each statement.

1. Like human beings, angels have bodies.   True   False

2. Like human souls, angels are immortal.   True   False

3. The devil is an angel who turned against God.   True   False

4. Angels watch over us and lead us to God.   True   False

5. Angels are mentioned all through the Bible.   True   False

6. When human beings die, they become angels.   True   False

7. Every person has an angel assigned to him.   True   False

8. Man has a stronger will and greater intellect than the angels.   True   False

9. Angels are pictured with wings because they are God's messengers.   True   False

10. Angels do not have free will; they are controlled by God.   True   False

Name the Angel

_____

1. The word "Saint" is often used before my name, but I am not a human being; I am an angel. I am called "archangel", which means I am a leader among the angels. If you see a picture of me, I am usually shown fighting a dragon; that means that I am in battle against the devil for your sake and for all the Church. My name means "God-like".

   Who am I? _____

2. I have been praying for you and helping you since you were very small. I am mentioned in the Bible, in Matthew 18:10 and in other places. Even before Jesus was born, the Jewish people believed in me and those like me. I am your special friend, and I will help you get to heaven.

   Who am I? _____

3. I too am an archangel. I have had the privilege of announcing some very important news to some very special people. I appeared to Zechariah to tell him that he would be the father of John, who would become John the Baptist. I told Mary that she had been chosen by God to bear his Son, Jesus. These stories are told in the Gospel of Luke.

   Who am I? _____

The Names of Jesus

NAME _____

Jesus Christ is—first and most important—our Savior, the Son of God, who became man so that he could save us from our sins and return to us the promise of heaven. Yet, in addition to knowing him as our Savior, we sometimes hear and speak of him with other titles and descriptions. Jesus and his followers gave us these other names so that we could more fully understand and think about his love for us.

Fill in the blanks in the sentences below using words from the list at right. Later, you can look for these titles when you are reading the Bible and listen for them in the prayers and readings of the Mass.

Good
Bread
Son
I Am
Adam
Light
Risen
Lord
Lamb
Man

1. Jesus always referred to God as his Father; therefore, he identifies himself as the _____ of God.

2. Because his obedience made up in a glorious way for the disobedience of the first man, Adam, Jesus is a kind of New _____.

3. During his public ministry, Jesus demonstrated through miracles (healings, calming the storm, raising the dead) that he is the _____, or master, of creation.

4. Jesus died, was buried, and rose from the dead. He is alive today as the _____ One, in whom we hope for our own resurrection.

5. In Holy Communion, Jesus is revealed by faith as the _____ of Life.

6. During the Passover, the Israelite slaves in Egypt killed a young sheep or goat and put its blood on their doorposts so that death would "pass over" them. Jesus became the new and perfect _____ of God by shedding his blood and "covering" all believers so that they would be spared from the slavery of sin and separation from God.

7. By calling himself the Son of _____, Jesus expressed the truth that he is fully human and came to serve mankind.

8. Jesus Christ "lay down his life for his sheep". He not only guides us and protects our souls from danger, he actually died so we could live. He is the _____ Shepherd.

9. Jesus is truly God, therefore, he can call himself by the name that God revealed to Moses: "Yahweh", or "_____".

10. Before Jesus came, the world was in spiritual darkness because of sin. Jesus is now the _____ of the world.

100 Activities Based on the Catechism of the Catholic Church
© 2013 Ignatius Press

The Consoler

NAME

In the Gospel of John, Jesus tells his followers about the Holy Spirit, who will come to them after Jesus goes to be with his Father. Jesus uses a special name to describe the Holy Spirit. The name means "he who is called to one's side", or "consoler". Discover this special name by filling in the blanks below and placing the boxed letters in order at the bottom of the page.

1. ☐ _ _ _ _ _ _ _ _

2. ☐ _ _ _ _ _ _ _

3. _ _ ☐ _

4. _ _ _ _ _ ☐ _

5. _ _ _ _ ☐ _

6. _ _ ☐ _
_ _ _ _ _ _

7. _ _ _ ☐ _

8. _ _ _ _ _ ☐ _ _ _

9. _ _ _ ☐

1. This feast marks the beginning of the Church, when the Holy Spirit came upon the disciples in the form of tongues of fire.

2. Through the power of the Holy Spirit, these chosen followers of Jesus were able to work healing miracles as Jesus did.

3. This faithful daughter of Israel was specially prepared by the Holy Spirit to become the Mother of God.

4. This great father of the faith experienced the power of the Holy Spirit with God's promise that he would be the father of a whole nation, even though he and his wife, Sarah, were childless.

5. We believe the Holy Spirit, in union with the Father and Son, guides the Catholic _____.

6. This Person of the Blessed Trinity came into your soul at your Baptism.

7. This symbol of the Holy Spirit is used in the Sacrament of Baptism and reminds us of being washed clean.

8. The Holy Spirit inspired the writing of, and continues to speak to us through, the Bible, also known as Sacred _____.

9. This traditional symbol of the Spirit is the form in which he appeared over Jesus after his Baptism.

The name Jesus used for the Holy Spirit is _ _ _ _ _ _ _ _ _.
1 2 3 4 5 6 7 8 9

The Fruits of the Holy Spirit

NAME _____

God pours out his love to us through the Holy Spirit, whom we received at our Baptism. It is through the Holy Spirit that our sins are forgiven and God's life in us can shine, bringing his love to others. Saint Paul wrote about nine ways that God's grace is evident in our lives. He called them the "fruits of the Spirit".

To illustrate how sin can cover up these fruits, the names of the fruits have been disguised in a code. Follow the instructions below to break through sin and reveal the fruits of the Spirit for all to see!

The code breaker at right is designed like the key pad of a phone. As you can see, most of the letters of the alphabet (except Q and Z) correspond to a number on the pad. The number alone won't tell you which letter to use in each group, however. So the code is as follows:

A number alone equals the first letter of a group (2 = A).
A number underlined equals the second letter (2 = B).
A number with a bar through it equals the third letter (2 = C).

Using this code, change the numbers to letters and name the fruits of the Spirit.

Phone Code		
	ABC	DEF
1	2	3
GHI	JKL	MNO
4	5	6
PRS	TUV	WXY
7	8	9
*	0	#

5 6 8 3   _____

5 6 9   _____

7 3 2 2 3   _____

7 2 8 4 3 6 2 3   _____

5 4 6 3 6 3 7 7   _____

4 6 6 3 6 3 7 7   _____

3 2 4 8 4 3 8 5 6 3 7 7   _____

4 3 6 8 5 3 6 3 7 7   _____

7 3 5 3 - 2 6 6 8 7 6 5   _____

The Four Marks of the Church

NAME _____

At each Sunday Mass, when we say the Nicene Creed, we state four things we believe about the Church. We say the Church is one, holy, catholic, and apostolic. These are the marks, or characteristics, of the Church. This activity will explore these four characteristics.

For each sentence, write the letter for the mark that best fits.

O = One   **H** = Holy   **C** = Catholic   **A** = Apostolic

_____ 1. The source of the Church is God himself, the mysterious unity of Three Persons in one God: Father, Son, and Holy Spirit.

_____ 2. Through the pope, bishops, and priests, the Church continues the mission Jesus gave his chosen followers: "As the Father has sent me, even so I send you."

_____ 3. Catholics all over the world profess the same faith.

_____ 4. The members of the Church, the People of God, are called saints.

_____ 5. Jesus invites all people to become fully his within the Catholic Church.

_____ 6. The Church canonizes certain of its members; that is, we recognize as models those Christians who practiced heroic virtue and faithfulness to God and who now dwell with him in heaven.

_____ 7. Where there are divisions among Christians, the Holy Spirit inspires us to pray and work for unity.

_____ 8. The Church is "universal" because she received from Christ all that is needed for salvation.

_____ 9. All members of the Church share in the work of the first Apostles to spread the good news of Christ.

_____ 10. The Church is sanctified by Christ.

_____ 11. Each particular Catholic church, that is, each diocese, is in communion with the Church of Rome.

_____ 12. The Holy Spirit dwells in the Church to ensure the continuous teaching Jesus gave to the Twelve.

The Church Is Apostolic / Names of the Apostles

TEACHER-DIRECTED ACTIVITY

Materials: board, chalk or markers and eraser, Bibles.

Purpose: to teach the fourth mark, apostolic, and names of the Apostles with memory aid.

Directions

Say:

When we say the Nicene Creed each Sunday, we recite what we call the four marks, or characteristics, of the Church. Say it with me: "I believe in one, holy, catholic and apostolic church." The Church is one, it is holy, it is catholic, and it is apostolic. [*Raise one finger for each mark as you say them.*] In this activity, we will focus on the fourth mark: apostolic. What word do you see inside this word "apostolic"? [*Write it out on the board. Listen for or provide the answer, apostle, and then write it directly underneath.*] What do the Apostles have to do with the Church? [*Affirm such answers as: They were chosen by Christ; they started the Church.*] Jesus built the Church beginning with the twelve Apostles. He asked them to follow him, he taught them about God and his plan to save the world through himself, and after he ascended to the Father he sent them the Holy Spirit so they could carry on his mission. Now that all the Apostles have died and are in heaven, who has taken their place? [*Listen for: priests, the pope, bishops.*] That's right, the bishops, together with the pope and assisted by priests—they are the successors of the Apostles, the ones who come after them to continue their work. That is why we say the Church is apostolic—it is founded on the Apostles and continues their mission. Every member of the Church shares in the apostolic mission, each in his own way.

Now, who can tell me the names of the twelve Apostles? Tell me as many as you can think of. [*Write them on board.*] I want to teach you a couple of tricks that may help you remember all twelve. For one, the names of the Apostles are all together in one place in the Gospel of Matthew, chapter 10, beginning with verse 2. Now, how will you remember that? Well, Matthew is an Apostle, and 10 plus 2 equals 12. Right now, let's look it up in our Bibles.

Now, here is the other trick. [*Write BAPTISM out on board, with space between and below the letters—see chart below.*] If you think of the "I" as "J", then all the names of the Apostles can fit into this word like an acrostic. Let's try it. Which Apostle's name starts with the letter "B"?

As students call out "Bartholomew", write it out underneath the "B". Continue this way until the board looks as shown below.

Give students time to copy this list in their notebooks or on paper. (Prior to that, if time allows, you may erase the Apostles' names, have students close their Bibles, and see how many they can remember on their own.)

B	A	P	T	I	S	M
Bartholomew	Andrew	Peter	Thomas	James	Simon	Matthew
		Philip	Thaddeus	James		
				John		
				Judas		

The Parts of the Mass

TEACHER-DIRECTED ACTIVITIES

Materials: board, chalk or markers, flashcards prepared from the next page.

Purpose: to increase students' understanding of the various elements in the Eucharistic celebration.

Activity A

To make flash cards, photocopy the next page onto heavy paper and cut apart. Or cut apart and paste onto index cards.

Make two columns on the board, labeling one "A" and the other "B". In each column write the following words, but list them in different order in each column:

> Homily
> Gathering
> Intercessions
> Penitential Rite
> Eucharistic Prayer
> Second Reading
> Liturgy of the Eucharist
> Rite of Peace
> Liturgy of the Word
> First Reading
> Offertory
> Preface Acclamation
> Memorial Acclamation
> Profession of Faith

Divide the class into two teams, A and B. Place chalk or marker near each column.

Say: Two students, one from each team, will come up to the board at a time. I will read a clue from one of these cards, and you try to identify which part of the

Mass I'm describing. The first one to circle the correct answer wins a point for his team. The team with the most points at the end is the winner. Be sure not to get excited and shout out the answer from your seats, or your team will lose the point. We'll take turns, so that for each clue, two different students will come up to the board.

After the game, tell the students that while the Liturgy has undergone changes over the years, the principal elements and order of the celebration have been the same since the first century! Read to them paragraph 1345 from the *Catechism of the Catholic Church*.

Activity B

Follow same directions as in Activity A except, instead of using cards, read from a missalette one of the prayers from a part of the Mass and have team members try to identify to which part of the Mass it belongs.

Activity C

Shuffle one set of the cards made for Activity A. Have student sort the cards into proper order.

HOMILY
After the Gospel reading, the priest or deacon gives a teaching about the Scriptures and encouragement to the people to put God's word into practice.

INTERCESSIONS
Just before we prepare for the Eucharist, we pray for the needs of the Church and the world.

EUCHARISTIC PRAYER
The summit, or peak, of the celebration, in which we give thanks to God, we ask his blessing on the gifts of bread and wine, and, with the words of Consecration, Christ becomes sacramentally present under the appearances of bread and wine.

LITURGY OF THE EUCHARIST
This section of the Mass includes the Preparation of the Gifts, the Lord's Prayer, the Breaking of the Bread, and Communion.

LITURGY OF THE WORD
This follows the "Glory to God" prayer and includes readings from the Scriptures.

OFFERTORY
The bread and wine are brought to the altar, and contributions to the church and for the poor are collected from those assembled.

MEMORIAL ACCLAMATION
This prayer, spoken by the people during the Eucharistic Prayer, is a remembrance of Jesus' death, Resurrection, and promise of his return.

GATHERING
Christians come together in one place to worship God and receive Christ in the Eucharist. This time is often celebrated with a song.

PENITENTIAL RITE
Before we listen to the Word of God, we make a prayer to confess our sins and ask the Lord's mercy.

SECOND READING
This is from one of the New Testament epistles.

RITE OF PEACE
The priest begins this with the words, "Lord Jesus Christ, who said to your apostles, Peace I leave you, my peace I give you."

FIRST READING
This comes from the Old Testament, the Acts of the Apostles, or Revelation.

PREFACE ACCLAMATION
Usually known as the "Holy, Holy, Holy", this prayer of praise and thanksgiving comes at the beginning of the Eucharistic Prayer.

PROFESSION OF FAITH
We say the words of the Nicene Creed, which begins, "I believe in one God."

Eucharist: Summit of Our Life in Christ

NAME _____

Write the answers to the following questions.

1. In attendance at a Catholic wedding are the bride's Uncle Henry, a practicing Catholic; the groom's co-worker Ed, who attends a Methodist church; and Charlene, a neighbor of the bride's family who has no religious beliefs. Of these three, who may receive Holy Communion at the Mass?

   _____

2. Two dispositions, or conditions, must be present before a person may receive Holy Communion. They are

   (a) freedom from _____ and (b) a _____ of one hour.

3. Holy Communion produces many good fruits in those who receive. Name one.

   _____

   _____

4. How often must a Catholic receive the Eucharist? _____

5. How often may a Catholic receive the Eucharist? _____

6. Why is the Mass sometimes referred to as "the Lord's Supper"?

   _____

7. What does it mean when we refer to "the Holy Sacrifice" or "Sacrifice of the Mass"?

   _____

8. During the Eucharistic Prayer, the priest says the words of Jesus that change the bread and wine into his Body and Blood. What are these words called?

   _____

9. The word "Eucharist" means "thanksgiving". For what do we give thanks when we celebrate the Mass?

   _____

10. Participating in the celebration of the Mass there may be the faithful, the priest, the deacon, the readers, extraordinary ministers of Holy Communion, and a cantor or musicians. Which of these **must** be there for a valid Mass?

    _____

11. Outside of the celebration of the Mass, how else do Catholics recognize the Real Presence of Christ in the Holy Eucharist?

    _____

Liturgical Colors

NAME

Our celebration of the Eucharist incorporates a variety of words, signs, symbols, and actions. One of these symbols is color. Liturgical colors symbolize the character of the different feasts and seasons of the Church year. These colors are used primarily in the priest's sacramental clothing, or vestments, and in the altar linens; they are also used on banners and other non-permanent decorations.

Below are the four colors in common liturgical use today, with their initials. Match the initial of the color to the descriptions given in Numbers 1 to 4. With that as a guide, match the initials with the feasts and seasons in which they are used, given in Numbers 5 to 13.

W = White   **R** = Red   **P** = Purple   **G** = Green

1. Sorrow for sin, repentance, preparation .... _____

2. Hope, growth, life .... _____

3. Joy, innocence, purity, virginity, victory .... _____

4. Sacrifice, blood sacrifice, zeal, Holy Spirit .... _____

   * * * * *

5. Advent .... _____

6. Sundays in Ordinary Time .... _____

7. Commemorations of Jesus' Passion .... _____

8. Feasts of Mary .... _____

9. Lent .... _____

10. Masses for martyrs .... _____

11. Christmas .... _____

12. Pentecost .... _____

13. Easter .... _____

Vocations: The Sacrament of Holy Orders

NAME

Activity A: Circle True or False

1. The sign of the Sacrament of Holy Orders is the laying on of hands by the bishop.   **True**   **False**

2. In imitation of Christ and of his twelve Apostles, who chose men as successors, only men may be ordained.   **True**   **False**

3. When a priest retires from active service, he ceases to be a priest.   **True**   **False**

4. Deacons are allowed to assist the priest and bishop by blessing marriages.   **True**   **False**

5. The three degrees of ordination are episcopate (bishop), presbyterate (priest), and diaconate (deacon).   **True**   **False**

6. Christ is present to the Church in the service of a priest, even if the priest commits a serious sin.   **True**   **False**

7. The bishop is the pastor of a particular church, which may include several parishes.   **True**   **False**

8. Priests exercise their ministry separately from the bishop in their own churches.   **True**   **False**

9. Women may one day be priests.   **True**   **False**

10. The work of a priest is to serve the faithful by teaching, offering the Sacrifice of the Mass, and leading souls to heaven.   **True**   **False**

11. A religious brother is like a nun, except he is ordained.   **True**   **False**

12. Recipients of the Sacrament of Holy Orders receive a special grace of the Holy Spirit, so they can act as a representative of Christ.   **True**   **False**

Activity B: Write an Essay

Imagine that a friend of yours who is not a Catholic asks you about our priests. Why do Catholics have priests? What are their responsibilities? Why would someone want to be one? How does someone know if God wants him in the priesthood? Write an essay to answer his questions.

Vocations: Following Christ's Call

NAME

Choose the best answer: write its letter (**a, b, c**) in the blanks.

1. Jesus Christ calls ____ to follow him.
   (a) Catholics
   (b) everyone
   (c) the baptized

2. The first people to be called by God were ____.
   (a) Peter and Andrew
   (b) Abraham and Sarah
   (c) Adam and Eve

3. The Lord is calling us to be _____.
   (a) holy
   (b) friendly
   (c) rich

4. Because the Church is ____, all people are invited to belong.
   (a) holy
   (b) apostolic
   (c) catholic

5. Every person can pray and listen for God's invitation to ____.
   (a) Holy Orders
   (b) the priesthood
   (c) a vocation

6. The main choices for an individual's vocation are to be ____.
   (a) priest or prophet
   (b) priest, religious, or married
   (c) holy or ordinary

7. Those who choose the consecrated life of a religious brother, sister, or priest live by the three evangelical counsels: ____.
   (a) faith, hope, and love
   (b) peace, humility, and joy
   (c) chastity, poverty, and obedience

8. The vocation of the ____ involves bringing Christ into the world of business, government, education, mass media, and so forth.
   (a) laity
   (b) bishops
   (c) religious

9. The work of a religious brother or sister may include ____.
   (a) being the mayor of a city
   (b) praying, teaching, or caring for the sick
   (c) raising a family

10. The Sacrament of Holy Orders is conferred upon _____.
    (a) bishops, priests, and deacons
    (b) popes, cardinals, and priests
    (c) priests, brothers, and sisters

11. The Sacrament of _____ confers an indelible spiritual character, which means it cannot be repeated and it lasts forever.
    (a) Holy Orders
    (b) Matrimony
    (c) Anointing of the Sick

12. The primary tasks of a married couple are_____.
    (a) making lots of money
    (b) assisting the pastor of the local parish
    (c) mutual love and the procreation and education of children

100 Activities Based on the Catechism of the Catholic Church
© 2013 Ignatius Press

The Family and Society

NAME

_____

God did not place you on the earth by yourself. He gave you a family.

Your own family might be large or it might be small, but whatever its size, your family is important. Families are the foundation for all of human society.

Fill in the blanks to see how your family is a building block of the Church and society.

My parents' names are

_____   _____

My name is

_____

My brothers and sisters are

_____   _____

_____   _____

We live at

_____

in the parish of _____   in the city of _____

in the diocese of _____   in the state of _____

We are members of the _____ Church.

We are citizens of the country of

_____

The Domestic Church

NAME

Each Christian family is an image of God, who is a communion of three Persons: Father, Son, and Holy Spirit. Each Christian family is a domestic church, or home church—a small community of believers who love and serve Christ by loving and serving one another.

Unscramble these words and phrases to show ways your family can fulfill its calling as a domestic church.

1
RYPA HAEC YDA

2
OG OT SAMS

3
DRAE HTE BBEIL

4
VELO ENO RHEAOTN

5
YEOB NSTREPA

6
CAHET RNLECHDI

7
EBECLEART GOTERHET

100 Activities Based on the Catechism of the Catholic Church
© 2013 Ignatius Press

The Fourth Commandment

NAME
_____

The Fourth Commandment gives us the standard for how we are to
treat one another within our family. The Fourth Commandment states:

_____ **your** _____ **and your** _____.

God promised that those who obeyed this commandment would be
blessed with a life of peace and well-being. Look up Exodus 20:12 for
the words of this promise and write them here:

_____

_____

List four ways you can honor your parents:

1. _____

   _____

2. _____

   _____

3. _____

   _____

4. _____

   _____

The Ten Commandments: A Scriptural Review

NAME

Printed below is a passage from Scripture that contains the Ten Commandments given to Moses by God on Mount Sinai. This passage is found in the second book of the Bible, the Book of Exodus, chapter 20, verses 2 to 17. Using red and black markers, pencils, or pens, identify each of the Ten Commandments in the Scripture passage in the following ways:

First Commandment:	Circle it.
Second Commandment:	Put a row of dots (. . .) under it.
Third Commandment:	Draw a box ☐ around it.
Fourth Commandment:	Put an X at beginning and end of it.
Fifth Commandment:	Put a + at beginning and end of it.
Sixth Commandment:	Draw a cloud around it.
Seventh Commandment:	Trace with red marker over its words.
Eighth Commandment:	Enclose it in parentheses ( ).
Ninth Commandment:	Underline it in red.
Tenth Commandment:	Underline it in black.

Hint: *The Commandments may be part of a sentence, an entire sentence, or a part of one sentence and all of another. Look hard.*

I am the Lord your God, who brought you out of the land of Egypt, out of the house of bondage. You shall have no other gods before me. You shall not make for yourself a graven image, or any likeness of anything that is in heaven above, or that is in the earth beneath, or that is in the water under the earth; you shall not bow down to them or serve them; for I the Lord your God am a jealous God, visiting the iniquity of the fathers upon the children to the third and the fourth generation of those who hate me, but showing steadfast love to thousands of those who love me and keep my commandments. You shall not take the name of the Lord your God in vain; for the Lord will not hold him guiltless who takes his name in vain. Remember the sabbath day, to keep it holy. Six days you shall labor, and do all your work; but the seventh day is a sabbath to the Lord your God; in it you shall not do any work, you, or your son, or your daughter, your manservant, or your maidservant, or your cattle, or the sojourner who is within your gates; for in six days the Lord made heaven and earth, the sea and all that is in them, and rested the seventh day; therefore the Lord blessed the sabbath day and hallowed it. Honor your father and your mother, that your days may be long in the land which the Lord your God gives you. You shall not kill. You shall not commit adultery. You shall not steal. You shall not bear false witness against your neighbor. You shall not covet your neighbor's house; you shall not covet your neighbor's wife, or his manservant, or his maidservant, or his ox, or his ass, or anything that is your neighbor's.

The Ten Commandments

NAME

As you know, the Ten Commandments are in the second book of the Bible, called Exodus. The Ten Commandments are also found in the fifth book of the Bible. The name of this book means "second law", because the book restates and explains the law God gave Moses on Mount Sinai. Both books are part of the Pentateuch, the first five books of the Bible, which hold special significance for the Jews because they contain all of the laws revealed to them by God.

What is the name of this book? _____

Find the Ten Commandments in chapter 5, verses 6 to 21, and read them aloud.

Discuss:

1. What did God do for the people of Israel, from whom he demands allegiance and love?

2. What does it mean to take God's name in vain?

3. Why were God's children told to keep holy the sabbath day?

4. What are some ways people might break the Fifth Commandment, without actually taking someone's life?

5. What does it mean to "bear false witness"?

6. God commands us not to "covet" things and people. What does it mean to covet, and what harm can come from it?

The Conscience: God's Voice Within

The *Catechism of the Catholic Church* defines "conscience" as "a judgment of reason whereby the human person recognizes the moral quality of a concrete act that he is going to perform, is in the process of performing, or has already completed." In other words, each person's conscience operates as an "inner voice" that helps him to know, and choose, right from wrong. Just as our bodies and minds grow, we must also allow our consciences to grow, by nourishing them with the food of prayer, reading of Holy Scripture, and attention to the truths of our Catholic faith.

Using the following clues, complete the puzzle below.

1. Because God gave us free will, we can freely _____ right or wrong.
2. If we are sure of what our conscience tells us, we must _____ it.
3. Conscience speaks to us as an _____ voice; in order to hear it, we should take time to quiet ourselves in prayer and self-examination.
4. The Holy _____ guides us in the formation of our conscience.
5. Another aid to forming our conscience is the Ten _____.
6. This word means not to know something, to be unaware. This state can cause our conscience to make poor judgments.
7. One rule for choosing rightly is never to do _____, even if good can come of it.
8. _____ is that which offends God; it also offends against a right conscience.
9. The teaching of the _____ can help us form a correct conscience.
10. We need a well-formed conscience in order to _____ God and one another.

1. [C] __ __ __ __ __
2. [O] __ __ __
3. __ [N] __ __ __
4. [S] __ __ __ __ __
5. [C] __ __ __ __ __ __ __ __ __ __ __ __
6. [I] __ __ __ __ __ __ __ __ __
7. [E] __ __ __
8. __ __ [N] __
9. [C] __ __ __ __ __
10. __ __ __ [E]

100 Activities Based on the Catechism of the Catholic Church
© 2013 Ignatius Press

Growing with the Gifts of the Spirit

NAME _____

At times it seems difficult, if not impossible, to follow Christ and his commandments. We are attracted to his goodness and love, and we want to grow strong in virtue, but we are weak and tempted to sin. How can we do what God asks of us?

Certainly we cannot do it on our own strength, and, fortunately, God does not expect us to. One of the ways he helps us is through the gifts of the Holy Spirit. The very nature of a gift is that it is free and unearned; so it is with these seven gifts. They came to you at your Baptism and will be strengthened in you when you receive the Sacrament of Confirmation. These gifts help us primarily by preparing our hearts to obey God.

For each gift listed, look up the Scripture reference given. Write the best definition you can find for it in your dictionary. Then, write down a made-up situation that a young person like yourself might face in which the gift could be of help.

1. Wisdom (Job 28:20–28)

Definition _____

Situation _____

2. Understanding (1 Kings 3:4–14)

Definition _____

Situation _____

3. Counsel (Psalm 16:7–11)

Definition _____

Situation _____

4. Fortitude (Psalm 18:2–4, 32–35)

Definition _____

Situation _____

5. Knowledge (Colossians 1:9–13)

Definition _____

Situation _____

6. Piety (1 Timothy 6:11–16)

Definition _____

Situation _____

7. Fear of the Lord (Proverbs 8:13, 9:10, 14:26–27)

Definition _____

Situation _____

Loving Your Brothers and Sisters

NAME

If God has given you brothers or sisters, they are a blessing that is easy to take for granted; or, at times, a blessing you may wish you didn't have! You really do love your siblings; but, because of original sin, they (and you) may not be always easy to live with. By following Christ, you can learn patience with and appreciation for your brothers and sisters. You can be the one to go the extra mile. Then you will be doubly blessed! If you don't have any siblings, you have opportunities to love your cousins, neighbors, and friends. They are blessings, too.

Read each situation below, and imagine yourself as the person involved. How would you respond? What Beatitudes, Commandments, or examples from Christ's life can apply? Write out your answers, then discuss them as a class.

1. Joseph's little sister asks for help with her math problems. Joseph was just getting ready to go outside to play ball. He is afraid that if he doesn't go now, the kids will start the game without him. What would you do if you were Joseph?

   _____

   _____

2. Jack's brother accidentally broke one of his trophies. Jack knows his brother doesn't have the money to replace it. What would you do if you were Jack?

   _____

   _____

3. Twin sisters Tara and Tina tried out for the cheerleading squad. Tara was chosen, but Tina wasn't. One of Tara's shoes has a hole in it, and she asks to borrow Tina's shoes for the first cheerleading practice. What would you do if you were Tina?

   _____

   _____

   _____

4. Michelle is crying in her room because she and her best friend got into an argument. Her sister, Renée, has missed spending time with Michelle, who is always with her friend. What would you say if you were Renée?

   _____

   _____

   _____

5. Peter and Theresa want to give their mother a gift for Mother's Day. Peter wants to pool their money and buy her a gift; Theresa wants to make something for her instead. They cannot agree. Choose either Peter or Theresa—what would you do?

   _____

   _____

   _____

   _____

The Works of Mercy

NAME

Jesus taught us fourteen specific and important ways we can love others. Seven have to do with meeting people's physical needs, so they are called "corporal", which means "of the body". The other seven have to do with the spirit, and therefore are called "spiritual".

Jesus gives everlasting life to those who do these things. (Read the Gospel of Matthew 25:31–46.)

There are small ways and big ways for us to do these good works in our lives. Pick three works of mercy from each category and write out the ways you can do these yourself.

Corporal Works of Mercy:

1. Feed the hungry
2. Give drink to the thirsty
3. Clothe the naked
4. Visit the imprisoned
5. Shelter the homeless
6. Visit the sick
7. Bury the dead

1. *I can* _____

 by _____

 _____

2. *I can* _____

 by _____

 _____

3. *I can* _____

 by _____

 _____

Spiritual Works of Mercy:

1. Admonish the sinner
2. Instruct the ignorant
3. Counsel the doubtful
4. Comfort the sorrowful
5. Bear wrongs patiently
6. Forgive injuries
7. Pray for the living and the dead

1. *I can* _____

 by _____

 _____

2. *I can* _____

 by _____

 _____

3. *I can* _____

 by _____

 _____

Praying for Others

_____

The type of prayer called "intercession" is defined as "asking on behalf of another" (CCC 2635). Look up and read aloud these Scriptures from the New Testament as examples of how the early Christians used intercession in their daily lives:

Acts 12:5–12	2 Thessalonians 3:1–2
2 Corinthians 1:11	1 Timothy 2:1–2
Ephesians 6:18–20	James 5:13–16

We, too, want to help others by praying for them, just as we hope to be prayed for in our times of need. This activity will help us to be more constant in our prayers for each other.

Activity A: For the family

Dedicate each of the seven days of the week to one member of the family. Every week on that day, everyone in the family can pray for that one individual. Any kind of prayer will do—the Rosary, an Our Father, a Hail Mary, mealtime prayers, or prayers through the day: "Dear Lord, help Mom get well", or "Please help Dad find work."

If you have more than seven in your family, you can pray for Mom and Dad together on one day, or double up the children on the weekdays. If you have fewer than seven family members, you can pray for grandparents, other close relatives, or friends on the extra day or days.

Fill out these lines with the names of your loved ones (don't forget yourself!), and bring this home to your family to discuss and share. Post it somewhere everyone can see and remember.

On Sunday we pray for _____

On Monday we pray for _____

On Tuesday we pray for _____

On Wednesday we pray for _____

On Thursday we pray for _____

On Friday we pray for _____

On Saturday we pray for _____

Activity B: For the class

As every month has at least 28 days, dedicate each day from 1 to 28 to a member of the class, or, for a small class, dedicate two days a month for each student. If you have extra days left over, you can use those to pray for your pastor, other parish priests, the director of religious education, and any others you can think of who need someone to pray for them—unborn children, the poor, the sick, and so forth. Discuss the possibilities as a class, and your teacher can write up a list to send home, so that you can add your classmates and others to your own daily prayers. God will be pleased as we pray for one another and grow together in his love!

The Five Forms of Prayer

All the years that you have been growing up and learning about your faith, your parents, teachers, pastor, and others have encouraged you to pray. You know prayer is a very important part of being a Christian. What exactly does it mean to pray? Is it saying the prayers you have memorized? Is it asking God for help? Is it being attentive at Mass?

Prayer is all of those things, and more.

Imagine your family suffered a big financial loss. You did not have the money to pay your bills or to buy food, and you would have to move out of your house. Suddenly, from out of nowhere, a man started mailing your family all the money you needed for everything and even more. You knew it was real, because you could see the house, the food, the clothes, and the special things you never had before. Naturally, you would want to meet this man. Who was he and why had he done this kindness, you would wonder. You probably would want to say thank you. You might ask your parents for his phone number, or you might write him a letter.

Suppose, though, that you let some time pass and did not get around to corresponding with the man who helped you. Maybe you hoped your parents would thank him for you. After a while, you stopped thinking about him. You never found out what kind of person he was. You never became his friend.

Without prayer, our faith in God can be like that. We know he is there and deserves our love, yet we neglect to communicate with him. Fortunately for us, God is more than a kind man, and he never stops reaching out to us in friendship. It is never too late to begin to pray.

Holy Scripture and apostolic Tradition have revealed five basic forms of prayer:

Blessing and adoration—*returning to God the love we receive from him, and giving him the worship he deserves as our King and Maker.*

Petition—*asking God for every need, especially for forgiveness and the coming of Christ's Kingdom, but also for every personal need, small or large.*

Intercession—*praying on behalf of others, even enemies.*

Thanksgiving—*thanking God for all good things and in every situation.*

Praise—*giving glory to God not because of what he does, but because of who he is.*

* * *

On a separate paper, write out the words to the Scripture passages named below. Identify which prayer form the verse describes or is an example of, and write the **name of the form** next to the verse.

1. Luke 18:13
2. 1 Thessalonians 5:18
3. Psalm 8:1
4. Ephesians 1:3
5. Psalm 9:1
6. 2 Thessalonians 1:11
7. 1 Peter 1:3
8. Revelation 19:1
9. Acts 7:59–60
10. James 1:5

Prayers in the Holy Liturgy

NAME

The Church teaches us that there are **five forms of prayer**: blessing and adoration, petition, intercession, thanksgiving, and praise. We find these forms in the Sacred Scriptures, in our personal communion with God, and in the Mass.

In this exercise, there are three columns. On the left is a phrase from one of the prayers in the Mass. In the center, you are to write the name of the prayer or specific part of the Mass from which the phrase comes. You may refer to a missalette to find the phrases. Then, on the right, identify the **prayer form** of which the given phrase is an example. (The first is done for you.)

Phrase	Prayer / Part of Mass	Form
1. Alleluia, alleluia, alleluia.	*Gospel Acclamation*	*praise*
2. Deliver us, Lord, we pray, from every evil, graciously grant peace in our days . . .		
3. Blessed are you, Lord God of all creation, for through your goodness we have received the bread we offer . . .		
4. We pray to the Lord: Lord, hear our prayer.		
5. May almighty God have mercy on us, forgive us our sins, and bring us to everlasting life.		
6. It is truly right and just, our duty and our salvation, at all times to acclaim you, O Lord . . .		
7. For you alone are the Holy One, you alone are the Lord, you alone are the Most High, Jesus Christ . . .		
8. Lamb of God, you take away the sins of the world, have mercy on us.		
9. Blessed is he who comes in the name of the Lord.		
10. Through him, and with him, and in him, O God, almighty Father, in the unity of the Holy Spirit, all glory and honor is yours . . .		

100 Activities Based on the Catechism of the Catholic Church
© 2013 Ignatius Press

Giving Thanks: Counting Your Blessings

NAME

When we think of praying, we often think of asking God for things we want or need. This kind of prayer, called "petition", is only one type of prayer. There are four others: blessing and adoration, intercession, praise, and thanksgiving. This exercise will focus on the prayer of thanksgiving.

At every Mass, we give thanks together: the word "Eucharist" means "thanksgiving". During his ministry on earth, Jesus gave thanks to his Father (Mt 11:25–27), and Saint Paul instructed the early Christians to "give thanks in all circumstances" (1 Thess 5:18).

For what can we give thanks? Everything! We can thank God even for difficulties, knowing that he will bring good out of them. When can we give thanks? Anytime, whether it be after receiving Holy Communion, when we wake up in the morning, or when we go to sleep at night.

God gives us so many good things that sometimes we take them for granted; that is, we expect them and forget to see them as gifts. Making a list of your blessings may help you to see all the good God has done for you. Make a silent prayer as you list your blessings below:

Thank you, God, for these spiritual gifts (*for example, Holy Communion, forgiveness*) . . .

_____

_____

_____

_____

Thank you, God, for these special people (*for example, parents, parish priest, friends*) . . .

_____

_____

_____

_____

_____

Giving Thanks: Counting Your Blessings

NAME _____

Thank you, God, for creating me as you did (that is, with my senses, abilities, gifts) . . .

_____

_____

_____

_____

Thank you, God, for the beautiful world you made (that is, for plants, for pets, for places I have seen or read about) . . .

_____

_____

_____

_____

Thank you, God, for this special prayer you answered . . .

_____

_____

_____

_____

Thank you, God, for bringing good out of this bad situation . . .

_____

_____

_____

_____

This list is for you alone. You may choose to keep it and even add to it.

Praying with the Psalms

NAME

The *Catechism of the Catholic Church* describes the Psalms as "the masterwork of prayer in the Old Testament". Incorporated into the Mass, the Psalms are a part of our communal, or shared, prayer in the Church. The Psalms are also perfectly suited for personal prayer, speaking as they do with genuine human emotion and a simplicity that transcends place and time.

This exercise is intended to help you examine the Psalms in order to increase your appreciation of the Psalm prayers at Mass and in your personal prayers. Read each of the following three passages from the Book of Psalms, and answer the questions.

1. **PSALM 23:1–6**

    a. Where else in the Bible (generally) do we hear God described as a shepherd?

    _____

    b. If the Lord is my shepherd, what does that make me?

    _____

    c. Why is that a good description?

    _____

    _____

    d. Describe the mood of this Psalm.

    _____

    _____

2. **PSALM 22:2–22**

    a. This Psalm opens with a very different mood from that of Psalm 23. Describe it.

    _____

    _____

    _____

Praying with the Psalms

NAME

b. Read verses 1 and 17. Of what incident in the Gospels do these remind you? What other verse(s) remind you of this?

_____

_____

c. Many images are used to describe the Psalmist's suffering—bullocks, lions, the sword, and so on. Which image speaks strongly to you, and why?

_____

_____

_____

3. PSALM 96:1–13

a. This Psalm is an example of which form of prayer (blessing and adoration, thanksgiving, petition, intercession, praise)?

_____

b. Was this Psalm likely intended for an assembly or an individual? Why do you think so?

_____

_____

c. This exultation mentions many different attributes of God. Name several of them.

_____   _____

_____   _____

_____   _____

_____   _____

The Rosary

The Rosary is the most loved of all the special prayers we pray to Mary, the Mother of God and our Mother. The Rosary was revealed to Saint Dominic by Mary herself. Since then, many popes, holy people, and the Blessed Mother have urged Christians to pray the Rosary.

The complete Rosary consists of fifteen decades (a decade is one Our Father, ten Hail Marys, and one Glory Be). As you pray each decade, you are to think about a mystery, or special event, in the life of Jesus or Mary. The mysteries are grouped into three sets: the **Joyful**, the **Sorrowful**, and the **Glorious**. In 2002, Pope John Paul II added as an option the Luminous Mysteries.

Activity A: Below, in the left column, are the names of the mysteries of the Rosary. The right column contains brief descriptions of each mystery. Write the letter of the description next to the name of the correct mystery.

Joyful Mysteries (Monday, Thursday, Saturday)

_____ 1. The Annunciation

_____ 2. The Visitation

_____ 3. The Nativity

_____ 4. The Presentation

_____ 5. The Finding in the Temple

Sorrowful Mysteries (Tuesday and Friday)

_____ 6. The Agony in the Garden

_____ 7. The Scourging at the Pillar

_____ 8. The Crowning with Thorns

_____ 9. The Carrying of the Cross

_____ 10. The Crucifixion

Glorious Mysteries (Wednesday and Sunday)

_____ 11. The Resurrection

_____ 12. The Ascension

_____ 13. The Descent of the Spirit

_____ 14. The Assumption

_____ 15. The Coronation

Luminous Mysteries (optional for Thursday)

_____ 11. The Baptism in the Jordan

_____ 12. The Wedding at Cana

_____ 13. The Proclamation of the Kingdom

_____ 14. The Transfiguration

_____ 15. The Institution of the Eucharist

A. *Jesus gives his Body and Blood to his disciples.*

B. *Jesus is tied to a pole and whipped.*

C. *Jesus is born in Bethlehem.*

D. *Mary is crowned Queen of Heaven and Earth.*

E. *The angel Gabriel appears to Mary and tells her that she is to be the Mother of God.*

F. *Jesus appears in a heavenly form to Peter, James, and John*

G. *Jesus suffers the night before he is to die.*

H. *This event is also known as Pentecost.*

I. *Jesus rises from the dead.*

J. *Jesus calls people to believe in the gospel.*

K. *Jesus is nailed to the Cross and dies.*

L. *In accordance with the law, Mary and Joseph present Jesus in the Temple.*

M. *The Spirit descends on Jesus like a dove.*

N. *Forty days after his death, Jesus goes up into heaven to be with the Father.*

O. *Jesus is made to carry his Cross to Calvary.*

P. *Mary goes to see her cousin Elizabeth, who is also with child.*

Q. *After Jesus is lost for three days, Mary and Joseph find him in the Temple.*

R. *A crown of thorns is placed on Jesus' head.*

S. *Jesus turns water into wine at Mary's request.*

T. *After her life on earth is complete, Mary is brought up into heaven by Jesus.*

The Rosary, cont'd

NAME

Activity B

Connect the letters from Activity A **in their final order** to solve the dot-to-dot puzzle. (Hint: start with E.)

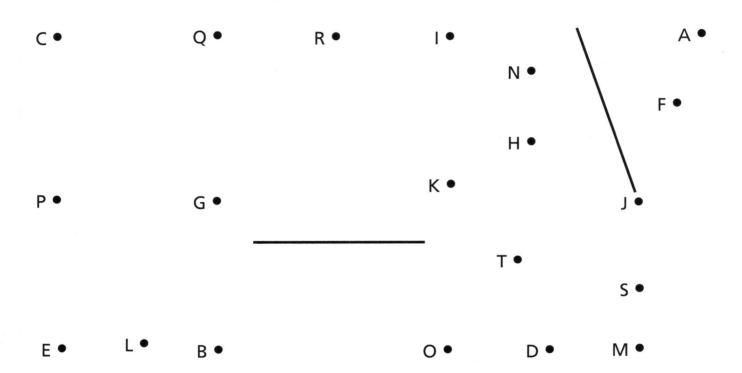

Activity C

Read the Bible verses indicated below, and, using Activity A as a reference, write the name of the mystery of the Rosary described in the verses, and from which set of mysteries it comes.

1. Matthew 3:13–17 _____ from the _____ mysteries.

2. Luke 24:1–9 _____ from the _____ mysteries.

3. Luke 1:26–31 _____ from the _____ mysteries.

4. Matthew 26:36–39 _____ from the _____ mysteries.

100 Activities Based on the Catechism of the Catholic Church
© 2013 Ignatius Press

The Hail Mary

NAME

Mary is the first Christian and the greatest saint. She was chosen for the most important role given to any created person in history, to be the Mother of Jesus, and she accepted God's will with all of her heart. We believe she is our Mother in heaven, and, as such, we pray to her, knowing that she loves us, and we pray with her, knowing that she brings our prayers to the heart of Jesus.

One of the Church's favorite ways to pray to Mary is the Hail Mary. This prayer not only asks for Mary's intercession for us, but also affirms several important truths about Mary and Jesus.

When we pray . . .

1. Hail, Mary

2. full of grace

3. the Lord is with thee

4. Blessed art thou among women

5. and blessed is the fruit of thy womb, Jesus

6. Holy Mary

7. Mother of God

8. pray for us sinners now

9. and at the hour of our death

Use these words to complete the sentences

original sin	true man
prayers	Elizabeth
the angel Gabriel	the Cross
conceived	personal sin
our Mother	heaven
the Mother of Jesus	faith
saint	the Holy Spirit

We remember that . . .

1. God sent this joyful greeting through _____ _____ _____, who announced that Mary was chosen to be _____ _____ ____ _____.

2. God prepared Mary for her role by creating her without _____ _____.

3. By God's grace, Mary remained free of _____ _____.

4. Mary's cousin _____ greeted Mary in this way to proclaim Mary's great _____ .

5. By the power of _____ _____ _____, Jesus was _____ inside Mary.

6. Mary is a _____.

7. Jesus is true God and _____ _____.

8. As _____ _____, Mary listens to our prayers and brings them, with her _____, to God.

9. Mary was present with Jesus at _____ _____. She will be with us, too, to lead us to _____.

Sing of Mary

No woman in history has been more revered or loved than Mary, Mother of Jesus and Mother of the Church. She is the model Christian, having said yes to God through the grace of Christ throughout her life. She is the Queen of All Saints and the patron saint of many countries, including the United States. Truly, as she proclaimed in the Magnificat, "All generations will call me blessed" (Lk 1:48).

The devotion we give to Mary is distinct from the adoration we give God. Though without sin, she remains a created being; God is our Creator and the only One whom we adore. Nevertheless, devotion to the Blessed Mother is not an add-on to our faith; rather, it flows naturally from our worship of Christ, her Son and Savior. When we extol Mary, we glorify Christ.

It is no surprise, then, that numerous hymns to and about Mary have been composed and sung over the centuries of Christian worship. They are sung on Marian feast days, other Masses in her honor, and at May crownings. New hymns have been written, and traditional ones remain.

Activity A

Check the index of your hymnbook(s) for titles that refer to Mary. Examples of some titles you may find are: "Immaculate Mary", "Hail, Holy Queen Enthroned Above", "Sing of Mary", "Song of Mary", "Virgin Full of Grace", "Daily, Daily Sing to Mary", "The Magnificat", "Hail Mary", "She Will Show Us the Promised One", "Mary's Song", "My Soul Magnifies the Lord", "Faithful Love", and "On This Day, O Beautiful Mother".

Note: For this activity, you will need a Catholic hymnal or two and writing materials for short answers.

Read through the lyrics of some of these Marian hymns. You may recognize some favorites, or you may find one you have not heard but whose lyrics you enjoy. Choose one hymn, and, on a separate paper, answer the following questions:

Is the song from, about, or addressed to Mary?

What titles for Mary are used (for example, Queen, Virgin)?

Which attributes of Mary are mentioned (for example, humility, beauty)?

Which attributes of God are mentioned?

Why did you choose this hymn, and what do you like about it?

Sing of Mary

NAME

Activity B

After reading through some of the Marian hymns (see Activity A), write your own song for Mary. (You don't have to write the music, or sing it!) Think about what titles for Mary you could emphasize, which aspects of her life you could highlight, or what requests you could make of her. How can your hymn give glory to God? Remember, a hymn is essentially a prayer in poem form, with regular stanzas. It may rhyme, but it does not need to.

Catholic Countdown

NAME

Numbers appear throughout the Bible and in our practice of the Catholic faith. As a brief review of some elements of the Faith you have been learning, fill in the blanks of these countdown sentences with words given in the list at right. (Not all the words in the list will be used.)

1. Jesus chose **12** men to _____ him and lead the Church as his _____.

2. Only **11** of these men were present at the descent of the Holy Spirit, called _____.

3. God gave Moses **10** _____, which still guide the Church in following Christ.

4. The traditional spiritual practice known as a _____ includes saying certain prayers for **9** days in a row.

5. The **8** _____, taught to us by Jesus, help us to act in ways that will bring us happiness with God now and in heaven.

6. Jesus instituted **7** _____, through which we receive grace.

7. God _____ the world out of _____ in **6** days.

8. The first **5** books of the Bible, known as the _____, are special to the Jewish people because they contain all of the _____ revealed to them by God.

9. The **4** Gospel writers are: _____, _____, _____, and _____.

10. The **3** Persons of the Blessed Trinity are the _____, the _____, and the _____.

11. All people are _____ of _____ and _____, the **2** people God placed in the Garden of _____.

12. We are made by, and for eternal life with, the **1** _____.

Pentecost
Commandments
Holy Spirit
Matthew
James
descendants
Beatitudes
Eve
Luke
John
novena
rosary
Adam
Father
Pentateuch
Apostles
Mark
pope
follow
True God
created
Eden
saved
Son
laws
sacraments
prayers
nothing

I Believe the Nicene Creed

The Nicene Creed, recited at every Sunday Mass, summarizes the most important beliefs of the Christian faith. A miniature catechism in itself, some of its components respond directly to certain heresies (denials of essential truths of faith) refuted by the bishops' councils of Nicaea and Constantinople in the fourth century. The Nicene Creed is sufficient to clarify many beliefs that can be contrasted not only with Christian heresy, but non-Christian religions as well.

On the second page of this exercise, match the letter of the doctrinal statement from the Nicene Creed in the left column with the heresy or non-Christian religious belief that it refutes in the right column. Some letters will be used more than once, others not at all.

I Believe the Nicene Creed

NAME

WHAT I BELIEVE

a. I believe in one God,
the Father almighty,

b. maker of heaven and earth,
of all things visible and invisible.

c. I believe in one Lord Jesus Christ,
the Only Begotten Son of God,
born of the Father before all ages.
God from God, Light from Light,
true God from true God,
begotten, not made,
consubstantial with the Father;
through him all things were made.

d. For us men and for our salvation
he came down from heaven,

e. and by the Holy Spirit
was incarnate of the Virgin Mary,
and became man.

f. For our sake he was crucified under
Pontius Pilate,
he suffered death and was buried,

g. and rose again on the third day
in accordance with the Scriptures.
He ascended into heaven and is seated
at the right hand of the Father.
He will come again in glory
to judge the living and the dead
and his kingdom will have no end.

h. I believe in the Holy Spirit,
the Lord, the giver of life,
who proceeds from the Father and
the Son,
who with the Father and the
Son is adored and glorified,
who has spoken through the prophets.

i. I believe in one, holy, catholic and
apostolic Church.

j. I confess one baptism
for the forgiveness of sins

k. and I look forward to the resurrection
of the dead and the life of the world to
come. Amen.

OTHER BELIEFS

_____ 1. The Messiah, the one anointed by God to save us from sin and death, has not yet come. (Judaism)

_____ 2. The world was not created by God but has always existed as matter. (Materialism)

_____ 3. Jesus is not one with or equal to God the Father. (Arianism, fourth century; also Islam, Mormonism, Jehovah's Witnesses)

_____ 4. Sins are not forgiven through the death of Jesus. (Judaism, Islam, Hinduism, Buddhism)

_____ 5. Jesus was merely a prophet, as were Moses, Muhammad, and others. (Islam)

_____ 6. There are many gods. (Hinduism)

_____ 7. Christ did not and could not suffer. (Transcendental Meditation)

_____ 8. After death a person is reincarnated, that is, his soul inhabits another body. (Buddhism, Hinduism, New Age)

_____ 9. Everything is God. (Pantheism, New Age)

_____ 10. Jesus did not have a human nature, only a divine nature in a human body. (Gnosticism)

_____ 11. Jesus did not rise from the dead. His disciples merely "kept him alive" by passing on his teachings. (Some modern biblical criticism)

_____ 12. Salvation results after experiencing multiple rebirths and reaching a state of peace called nirvana. (Hinduism, Buddhism)

Distinguishing the Creeds

TEACHER-DIRECTED ACTIVITY

Activity A

Divide the class into two teams. Recite aloud from one of the Creeds. The first team to identify correctly the Apostles' or the Nicene Creed earns a point. Keep score until several rounds have been played.

Activity B

Write or type out statements from the Creeds onto 20 different index cards (10 for each Creed). Shuffle the deck of cards. Students sort cards in order, in two rows, one for each Creed.

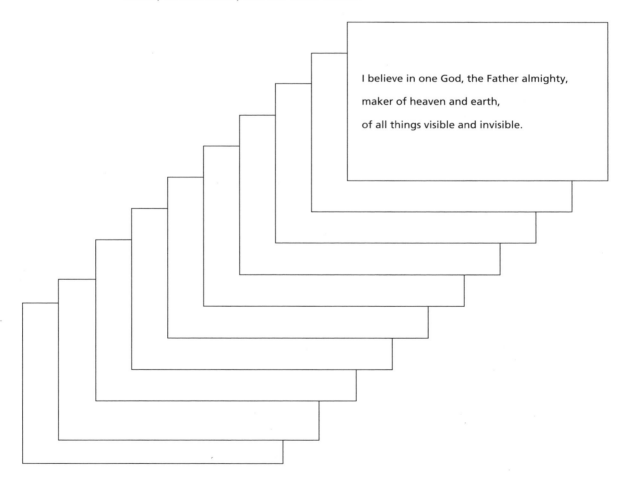

I believe in one God, the Father almighty,

maker of heaven and earth,

of all things visible and invisible.

The Various Books of the Bible

NAME

You have learned that the Bible is divided into two parts, the Old Testament and the New Testament. You probably are aware that the Old Testament contains the Book of Genesis and tells of Moses and David, while the New Testament features the life of Christ and the early Christians. Beyond that may be uncharted territory.

This exercise is intended to offer a basic map to help you begin to make your way through the 73 different but related books of the Bible and to see how they all fit together. Your travels will last well beyond this year—it can be a wonderful lifelong journey—but this should help get you started.

The Old Testament opens with five books (Torah in Hebrew), also called the **Pentateuch**, the most sacred writings of the Jewish religion. They include the story of creation and the great flood, the call of Abraham, the life of Moses, the freeing of the Israelites from slavery in Egypt, and the giving of God's laws in the desert.

After that come the **Historical Books**, which continue the story of the Israelites, beginning with the leadership of Joshua, successor to Moses. These books relate the kingship of David, the rebuilding of the Jewish homeland after exile in Babylon, and, finally, the rededication of the Temple. Tucked in with this history are the books of Ruth, Tobit, Judith, and Esther, each separate stories drawn from this historical period.

The **Wisdom Books**, so called because their purpose is to teach, are in the form of Hebrew poetry and concern the problem of suffering, virtuous living, and the value of wisdom. The lyrical style of the Psalms and the Song of Solomon (Song of Songs) place them in this category, although they are not wisdom literature as such. The Psalms are songs of prayer and worship; the Song of Solomon is a parable in the style of a love poem.

Placed at the end of the Old Testament are the **Prophetic Books**, the writings of God's spokesmen, the prophets. They include the major prophets—Isaiah, Jeremiah, Daniel, and Ezekiel—as well as the twelve minor prophets. The prophets were called by God throughout the history of Israel to preach repentance and, ultimately, to prepare the way for Christ.

Perhaps more familiar to you are the 27 books of the New Testament, beginning with the four **Gospels**. Next comes the Acts of the Apostles, which is a **History of the Early Church**, followed by the **Letters** written by Saint Paul and other apostles to various Christian individuals and communities.

The Bible closes with an **Apocalyptic Book**, a story that unveils, using rich symbolic language, a prophetic message from God about the ultimate triumph of good over evil.

The Various Books of the Bible

NAME

Look up the Scripture passages listed on the left. Determine which category given on the right that the book of the Bible belongs in, and write the letter in the space given.

1. Revelation 9:1–11 _____

2. Malachi 3:1–5 _____

3. Philippians 1:1–11 _____

4. 1 Samuel 17:41–51 _____

5. Proverbs 4:10–13 _____

6. 1 John 2:1–5 _____

7. Exodus 34:27–35 _____

8. Acts 12:1–11 _____

9. John 2:1–11 _____

10. Ezra 3:1–6 _____

Old Testament

a. The Pentateuch

b. The Historical Books

c. The Wisdom Books

d. The Prophetic Books

New Testament

e. The Gospels

f. The History of the Early Church

g. The Letters

h. The Apocalyptic Book

The Names of God

What is in a name? According to the Catechism of the Catholic Church, a "name expresses a person's essence and identity and the meaning of this person's life". So it is with God's name.

God revealed himself to Moses in the burning bush as "Yhwh", sometimes spelled out "Yahweh". This mysterious name means "I am he who is". Out of reverence, this name is not spoken by the Jewish people, who instead use the name "Adonai"—that is, "Lord", when reading aloud the Scriptures. Through the generations God's people have used other names—many of them linked with "Yahweh"—to highlight different aspects of God's character. In our Christian faith, we can see how these qualities are perfectly reflected in Jesus.

Activity A

Using your Bibles, match each name for God with the Scriptures where that name can be found.

____ 1. Yahweh Tsidkenu (*The Lord Our Righteousness*)

____ 2. Yahweh Shalom (*The Lord Our Peace*)

____ 3. Yahweh Rapha (*The Lord Heals*)

____ 4. Yahweh Yireh (*The Lord Provides*)

____ 5. Yahweh Shammah (*The Lord Is There*)

____ 6. Yahweh M'Kaddesh (*The Lord Who Sanctifies*)

____ 7. Yahweh Raah (*The Lord Our Shepherd*)

____ 8. Yahweh Sabaoth (*The Lord of Hosts**)
    *hosts = an army, or a great multitude

a. Ezekiel 48:35

b. Judges 6:22–24

c. Ezekiel 34:11–16

d. Jeremiah 23:5–6

e. Exodus 15:26

f. Leviticus 20:8

g. Genesis 22:14

h. 1 Samuel 17:40–47

Activity B

On a separate sheet of paper, write a paragraph explaining which of the above names of God appeals to you most, and why.

Images of the Church

NAME

What comes to mind when you hear the words "the Church"? Do you picture the celebration of the Mass? Your local parish and its building, people, or activities? The pope and bishops? The apostles, saints, and martyrs?

The Church is all of these and more. The *Catechism of the Catholic Church* defines the Church as "the People that God gathers in the whole world". This includes the Eucharistic assembly, the local community of believers, and all believers everywhere, on earth and in heaven.

The Church is also a mystery, composed of human and divine, visible and invisible parts. The Scriptures shed light on this mystery by using symbols and images based on everyday human experience to describe the Church. These include a sheepfold, a field prepared for growing, a temple, a bride, and a mother.

Activity A

At right are given the dominant images of the Church in the New Testament. Look up the Scriptures for each one, and complete the sentence with a quality of the symbol that applies to the Church.

The Body of Christ

Like a body, the Church . . .

1. John 6:55–56 _____
2. 1 Corinthians 12:12 _____
3. 1 Corinthians 12:14 _____
4. 1 Corinthians 12:18 _____
5. 1 Corinthians 12:26 _____
6. Ephesians 4:15 _____
7. Colossians 1:18 _____

The Bride of Christ

Like a bride, the Church . . .

8. Ephesians 5:25 _____
9. Ephesians 5:27 _____
10. Ephesians 5:29 _____

The Temple of the Holy Spirit

Like a temple, the Church . . .

11. 1 Corinthians 3:9 _____
12. 1 Corinthians 3:17 _____
13. 2 Corinthians 6:16 _____
14. Ephesians 2:20 _____
15. 1 Peter 2:6 _____

Activity B

Choose one of the images of the Church given above. On a separate sheet of paper, write a paragraph examining how the image suitably describes the Church. Develop the analogy; for example, if the Church is like a body, what is its food (Jn 6:55–56)? If it is a bride, who is the bridegroom? If it is a temple, who is the builder? Are there other characteristics in addition to those found in Scripture that also fit both the image and the Church?

The Consecrated Life

NAME _____

Among the various states in life to which a person may be called by God, the consecrated life offers many opportunities for a person to follow Christ intimately, and thus be a sign of our life in the world to come.

Read each clue, then unscramble the hidden words, which apply to the consecrated life.

1. Consecrated persons make a public profession—that is, a vow—to follow the three

   evangelical counsels, which are: _____, _____, and _____.

Y V R P E T O   T T S A H I Y C   E N E O B I D C E

2. Some consecrated persons live apart from the world in solitude, prayer, and penance. They

   are called _____.

M I S T R E H

3. A consecrated woman who is spiritually betrothed to Christ, and thus becomes a special sign

   of the Church's love for Christ, is called a _____.

I I N G V R

4. Consecrated persons who live together in a common fraternal life under a particular rule, or

   order, are called _____.

U L R I O S G I E

5. The word "consecrated" means to be "_____ _____ for holy use".

E T S   T R A A P

6. Many consecrated persons have been influential in the _____ work of the

S R A S I Y M N I O

   Church, that is, the spreading of the gospel to all the world.

7. Belonging to a secular institute is a way in which Christians can live a consecrated life

   while remaining in _____ _____ and working for its sanctification.

E H T   L W R O D

8. By consecrating himself more closely to God, a person also presents himself to the

   _____ for its good.

R H H C U C

9. Consecrated persons encourage others by their _____. They _____ that

P L X M E A E   E S T I S W N

   our true home is heaven, and the way there is Christ.

Patron Saints

TEACHER-DIRECTED ACTIVITY

Activity A: *Charade of Saints*

Materials: index cards, prepared with names from list on page 89; book of saints, such as *Butler's Lives of the Saints* or *The Picture Book of Saints* (Catholic Book Publishing); photocopies of list on page 89, one for each student.

Purpose: to acquaint students with the saints and remind them that these holy ones are alive in Christ and serve him by praying for us. A helpful resource would be a book on the saints, so that some general information can be given during the course of the game.

As the *Catechism* instructs us, the saints in heaven "contemplate God, praise him and constantly care for those whom they have left on earth. . . . We can and should ask them to intercede for us and for the whole world" (2683). Through the years, saints have become known for their special concern and effective prayers for certain persons, countries, or institutions.

Directions

Pass out index cards and lists, one of each per student.

Say: We are going to play a variation on the game Charades. Remember that the object of Charades is to guess what the player is acting out from the player's motions alone; he is not allowed to speak. Sometimes Charades is played with movie titles, books, or songs. Our game is going to be about patron saints.

Have you ever heard the word "patron"? [*It means someone who protects or helps another person; a benefactor.*]

What is a saint? [*A holy person declared by the Church to be in heaven because of his exemplary life on earth and the miracles worked through his prayers after his death; also, anyone who has died for the faith.*]

So then, what might a patron saint be? [*A holy person in heaven who cares for someone on earth.*]

Over the years, for different reasons, certain saints have come to be known as patron saints for certain people, institutions, or even things. Have you ever heard of praying to Saint Anthony to help you find a lost object? Or perhaps you've learned that Saint Patrick is the patron saint of Ireland, where he was a great missionary during his life. We can at any time ask any of the saints to pray for us, because that is their heavenly "work", to bring our prayers and needs to Christ, with whom they dwell in glory. But it is interesting to learn which saints are believed to have a special love for certain people and circumstances.

You have a list and an index card with names of some saints and those for whom they are patrons. When it is your turn to play, you act out what is on your card, either the saint or the person for whom the saint is a patron. The rest of the class must choose from the list which saint you are charading. For example, Saint Clare is the patroness of television. When Saint Clare consecrated herself to Christ, Saint Francis of Assisi cut off her hair. You could act out someone cutting hair; or you could act out a person watching television or making a TV show. When you've guessed the saint, please raise your hand and wait to be called on, then tell the class the name of the saint and that for which he is a patron—"Saint Clare, the patron saint of television." The first person to make a correct guess is the next player.

Choose a student to begin the game. Proceed as described. After a saint has been identified, you can share some interesting facts with the students such as when and where he lived, what miracles are associated with him, and so forth.

Patron Saints

NAME _____

Albert the Great (*scholar and bishop*) .... scientists

Anastasia (*martyr*) .... weavers

Andrew (*apostle*) .... fishermen

Ann (*mother of Mary*) ....homemakers

Apollonia (*martyr*) ....dentists

Barbara (*martyr*) .... prisoners, architects, and firefighters

Brendan (*missionary*) .... sailors

Catherine of Siena (*advised the pope*) .... nurses

Cecilia (*martyr*) .... musicians

Christopher (*carried the Christ Child*) .... motorists

Clare (*followed Saint Francis, founded Poor Clares*) .... television

Colette (*reformed the Poor Clares*) .... expectant mothers

Dorothy (*martyr*) .... florists and brides

Eligius (*goldsmith*) .... jewelers

Elizabeth of Hungary (*queen*) ....bakers

Frances Xavier Cabrini (*missionary to America*) .... immigrants

Francis de Sales (*bishop*) .... writers

Francis of Assisi (*founded the Order of Friars Minor, also known as
    Franciscans*) ....merchants and animals

Gabriel (*archangel*) .... mail carriers

Gemma (*mystic*) .... pharmacists

Gregory the Great (*pope*) ....singers and teachers

Isidore (*farmer*) .... farmers

Jerome (*Scripture scholar*) .... librarians

Joachim (*father of Mary*) .... fathers

Joan of Arc (*deliverer of France*) .... soldiers and France

Joseph (*foster father of Jesus*) .... carpenters

Joseph of Arimathea (*buried Jesus*) .... funeral directors

Lawrence (*martyr*) .... cooks

Louis of France (*king*) .... barbers

Lucy (*martyr*) .... eye patients

Lydwina (*united her sufferings with those of Christ*) .... skaters

Luke (*physician, Gospel writer*) .... doctors and artists

Matthew (*apostle*) .... accountants and bankers

Michael (*archangel*) ....police officers

Monica (*mother of Saint Augustine*) .... mothers

Sebastian (*soldier*) .... athletes and armies

Teresa of Avila (*reformed the Carmelite Order*) .... headache sufferers

Thérèse of Lisieux (*contemplative*) .... missionaries

Thomas Aquinas (*scholar*) ....students

Thomas More (*lawyer, martyr*) .... lawyers

Patron Saints

TEACHER-DIRECTED ACTIVITY

Activity B: *Who Am I?*

Materials: index cards and list of saints from Activity A; three holy cards of saints for prizes.

Directions

Tape an index card on the back of each student without letting the student see the name written on the card.

Say: Today we are going to play a game similar to a party game you may have played before. It's similar to Twenty Questions also. Please listen carefully to the directions. I am going to tape on each student's back an index card with the name of a saint. This is your secret identity. The object of the game is to be the first one to guess your identity.

Here's how you play. You mingle around the room and find another student to talk to. He looks at your card, and you look at his. You may ask him three questions about yourself that can be answered yes or no; for example, "Am I a man?" "Am I a priest?" "Did I found a religious order?" That student then may ask you three questions about his identity. Then you both find someone else to question. You continue in this manner until you can guess who you are. If you need help, I have posted a list of saints on the wall [or bulletin board] to give you some clues. When you have guessed correctly, come to me—the first three will get a little prize.

Activity C: *Saint Stories*

Materials: index cards from Activity A; books about the saints.

Directions

Distribute cards. Explain patron saints (see Activity A). Ask students to research a saint and write a short biography of his life.

The Resurrection and the Life

NAME

In a group of three or four, take turns looking up these definitions from the *Catechism of the Catholic Church*. Fill in the words being defined.

1. The end of earthly life; the consequence of sin (paragraphs 1007–8).

   _____

2. The reunion of our eternal souls with our transfigured bodies through the power of Christ at the end of time (paragraphs 997, 1001).

   _____

3. The sacrament through which we died and rose with Christ, and henceforth have already entered into his heavenly life (paragraphs 1002–3).

   _____

4. "Each man receives his eternal retribution in his immortal soul at the very moment of his death" (paragraph 1022). This is called the

   _____

5. The "ultimate end and fulfillment of the deepest human longings, the state of supreme, definitive happiness" (paragraph 1024).

   _____

6. "All who die in God's grace and friendship, but still imperfectly purified . . . undergo purification, so as to achieve the holiness necessary to enter the joy of heaven" (paragraphs 1030–31). This state is called

   _____

7. "To die in mortal sin without repenting and accepting God's merciful love means remaining separated from him forever by our own free choice" (paragraph 1033). This is

   _____

8. "In the presence of Christ, who is Truth itself, the truth of each man's relationship with God will be laid bare" (paragraph 1039). This hour is known as the

   _____

9. "Sacred Scripture calls [the] mysterious renewal, which will transform humanity and the world" at the end of time (paragraph 1043) two names:

   _____ and a _____

Articles Used in Worship

NAME _____

The signs and symbols of the Church's celebration of the supreme sacrament, the Sacrament of the Eucharist, include sacred clothing, books, and objects used in worship. Reflecting the long history of the Church, many of these liturgical articles have names with roots in the ancient languages of Latin and Greek.

See how many of the terms on the right you can correctly match with the descriptions on the left.

_____ 1. A square white cloth on which the chalice and paten are placed during Mass.

_____ 2. The priest's outer robe.

_____ 3. Decorative container used to display the Blessed Sacrament for adoration.

_____ 4. Long white tunic worn underneath other priestly vestments.

_____ 5. Person responsible for sacred objects and vestments.

_____ 6. Cloth used to wipe clean the chalice.

_____ 7. Instrument for sprinkling holy water.

_____ 8. Stiff square piece of cloth placed over the chalice during Mass. Also the cloth covering placed over the coffin at funeral Masses.

_____ 9. Strip of cloth worn over priest's shoulders; on a deacon, worn over the left shoulder and crossing to the right side.

_____ 10. Container used to carry Communion to the sick.

_____ 11. Container in which incense is burned.

_____ 12. Readings for the Mass organized by liturgical cycles.

_____ 13. A covered container for consecrated Hosts distributed at Mass or stored in the tabernacle.

_____ 14. Cord used to tie the alb.

_____ 15. Containers for water and wine brought to the altar at the Offertory.

_____ 16. Book used by the priest that contains prayers of the Mass.

_____ 17. Cup that holds the wine that becomes the Precious Blood.

a. alb

b. aspergillem

c. censer

d. chalice

e. chasuble

f. ciborium

g. cincture

h. corporal

i. cruets

j. lectionary

k. monstrance

l. pall

m. purificator

n. pyx

o. sacramentary

p. sacristan

q. stole

Lord, I Am Not Worthy

NAME _____

In 2011, the Catholic Church approved a revised English translation of the Holy Mass, to bring the text more in line with the official Latin Missal. For nearly fifty years English speakers have used a paraphrased translation. Now the English texts, like those of the other languages around the world, are a word-for-word translation. The result is more precision in meaning, closer alignment with the Scriptures, greater richness of theological concepts, and a more elevated tone.

One example of the updated direct translation is that, throughout the Mass, when the priest says, **"The Lord be with you"**, the response of the people used to be: "And also with you." Now we say: **"And with your spirit."** This more formal phrase is appropriate for the sublime occasion of the Mass. It also echoes the Scriptures, where similar greetings are offered: "The grace of the Lord Jesus Christ be with your spirit" (Phil 4:23) and "The Lord be with your spirit" (2 Tm 4:22) are some examples. Additionally, this wording demonstrates our belief that the Holy Spirit acts in a unique way through the priest, who by the grace of the Sacrament of Holy Orders has the power to change bread and wine into the Body and Blood of Christ.

For this activity, we will uncover the meaning of another seemingly simple wording change. During the Liturgy of the Eucharist, after we pray the "Lamb of God", we kneel, and the priest elevates the Host. We used to pray: "Lord, I'm not worthy to receive you, but only say the word, and I shall be healed." Now we pray:

> *Lord, I am not worthy that you should enter under my roof,*
> *but only say the word, and my soul shall be healed.*

In this new translation, we can now see the scriptural meaning of this prayer more clearly.

* * *

Read the Gospel of Matthew 8:5–13 and the Gospel of Luke 7:6–10 and answer the questions:

1. Which verses correspond to the prayer in the Mass? _____

2. Who is speaking to the Lord? _____

3. What is he asking of Jesus? To heal his _____ of _____

4. What does he believe about Jesus? _____

5. Does the Lord grant his request? _____

6. Does the Lord "come under his roof"? _____ Does he come under mine, and if so,

   how? _____

7. What am I asking of the Lord in this prayer? To heal my _____ of _____

8. Following this example in Scripture, what should my attitude be as I pray this prayer and

   approach Holy Communion? _____

Name Days

NAME

In many countries, a child's Name Day is as important a celebration as his birthday. A Name Day is the memorial day of a person's patron saint. If you share a first or middle name with a saint, that saint is your special guardian. Or, if your first or middle name is derived from that of a saint—for example, the names Maggie and Megan come from the name Margaret—that saint is your patron. If you do not know who your patron saint is or do not yet have one, choose a favorite saint to be your patron.

Using Church calendars and books about the saints, find your Name Day and write it here. Then write a paragraph about the life of your patron saint.

The Liturgy of the Hours

TEACHER-DIRECTED ACTIVITY

Materials: Liturgy of the Hours prayer books or booklets (one per student or one for every couple of students), available as *Christian Prayer* or *Shorter Christian Prayer*.

Purpose: to introduce students to the Divine Office, the prayer of the People of God. Praying the Liturgy of the Hours, though commonly associated with priests and religious as befits their calling, is also encouraged for "all the faithful as much as possible . . . either with the priests, or among themselves, or even individually" (*Sacrosanctum concilium*, 1963).

Directions

Invite your pastor to (1) give a guest lecture on the Liturgy of the Hours, to be followed by (2) his leading the students in daytime prayer. A chapel, if available, would be a desirable setting for the prayers; the actual prayer time should take about ten minutes. The priest (or you, with his guidance) will need to prepare materials ahead of time, by marking individual copies of the books so as to lead the students smoothly through the Office.

Questions for the pastor to answer in his lecture might include:

What is the Liturgy of the Hours?

Why is it the prayer of the Church?

Who prays it?

How is it prayed?

How often is it prayed, and how long are the prayers?

How can a layman make use of the prayers—in a family, in school, or as an individual?

What are the major components of the prayer? (*Psalms, Our Father, New Testament readings, and so on*)

Is it difficult to learn?

Why did the Church give us this guide rather than leave it to us to pray spontaneously through the day?

If your parish priest is not available, you could instead invite a deacon, religious brother or sister, or a layman educated and experienced in the use of the Liturgy of the Hours.

Important Days in the Liturgical Year

NAME

The Church calendar marks not the passage of time but various aspects of the Paschal mystery, that is, the mystery of Christ's life, death, and Resurrection. The Church begins a new liturgical year on the First Sunday of Advent. Included on the Church's calendar are solemnities, which celebrate the most significant events, people, and beliefs; feasts, or celebrations of secondary significance; and memorials, which honor martyrs and other saints.

Your teacher will give you a sample calendar with some dates circled to mark noteworthy liturgies, including solemnities, feasts, and memorials. For each liturgy named below, write the correct date from among those circled on the sample calendar. (Note: Some feasts and solemnities are "movable", that is, their date changes each year. For example, Easter's date is set according to natural cycles of the earth and moon and is adjusted yearly. Likewise, the dates for celebrations that are tied into Easter, such as Ash Wednesday and Ascension Thursday, also change. The date for Easter in this sample calendar is given as April 7.)

For a bonus: Put a star next to the dates of Holy Days of Obligation.

1. Easter   **April 7**   12. Assumption   _____

2. Christmas   _____   13. Saint Patrick's Day   _____

3. Christ the King   _____   14. Holy Family   _____
   (_last Sunday of liturgical year_)   (_Sunday after Christmas_)

4. First Sunday of Advent   _____   15. Solemnity of Mary   _____

5. Immaculate Conception   _____   16. Annunciation   _____

6. Pentecost (_"fiftieth day"_)   _____   17. Corpus Christi   _____
   (_second Sunday after Pentecost_)

7. Ascension Thursday   _____

8. Epiphany   _____   18. Holy Trinity   _____
   (_Sunday after Pentecost_)

9. Ash Wednesday   _____

    19. Birth of Mary   _____

10. Good Friday   _____   20. Sacred Heart   _____
    (_Friday after Corpus Christi_)

11. All Saints   _____

Important Days in the Liturgical Year

January

S	M	T	W	T	F	S
	①	2	3	4	5	6
⑦	8	9	10	11	12	13
14	15	16	17	18	19	20
21	22	23	24	25	26	27
28	29	30	31			

February

S	M	T	W	T	F	S
				1	2	3
4	5	6	7	8	9	10
11	12	13	14	15	16	17
18	19	20	㉑	22	23	24
25	26	27	28	29		

March

S	M	T	W	T	F	S
					1	2
3	4	5	6	7	8	9
10	11	12	13	14	15	16
⑰	18	19	20	21	22	23
24	㉕	26	27	28	29	30
31						

April

S	M	T	W	T	F	S
	1	2	3	4	⑤	6
⑦	8	9	10	11	12	13
14	15	16	17	18	19	20
21	22	23	24	25	26	27
28	29	30				

May

S	M	T	W	T	F	S
			1	2	3	4
5	6	7	8	9	10	11
12	13	14	15	⑯	17	18
19	20	21	22	23	24	25
㉖	27	28	29	30	31	

June

S	M	T	W	T	F	S
						1
②	3	4	5	6	7	8
⑨	10	11	12	13	⑭	15
16	17	18	19	20	21	22
23	24	25	26	27	28	29
30						

July

S	M	T	W	T	F	S
	1	2	3	4	5	6
7	8	9	10	11	12	13
14	15	16	17	18	19	20
21	22	23	24	25	26	27
28	29	30	31			

August

S	M	T	W	T	F	S
				1	2	3
4	5	6	7	8	9	10
11	12	13	14	⑮	16	17
18	19	20	21	22	23	24
25	26	27	28	29	30	31

September

S	M	T	W	T	F	S
1	2	3	4	5	6	7
⑧	9	10	11	12	13	14
15	16	17	18	19	20	21
22	23	24	25	26	27	28
29	30					

October

S	M	T	W	T	F	S
		1	2	3	4	5
6	7	8	9	10	11	12
13	14	15	16	17	18	19
20	21	22	23	24	25	26
27	28	29	30	31		

November

S	M	T	W	T	F	S
					①	2
3	4	5	6	7	8	9
10	11	12	13	14	15	16
17	18	19	20	21	22	23
㉔	25	26	27	28	29	30

December

S	M	T	W	T	F	S
①	2	3	4	5	6	7
⑧	9	10	11	12	13	14
15	16	17	18	19	20	21
22	23	24	㉕	26	27	28
㉙	30	31				

The Sacrament of Confirmation

NAME
_____

Circle the letter (**a, b, c**) of the correct answers.

1. Baptism, Eucharist, and Confirmation are united as the
   (a) Sacraments of Preparation
   (b) Sacraments of Initiation
   (c) Sacraments of Unification

2. Confirmation is necessary for a Christian because it
   (a) confers
   (b) replaces
   (c) completes
   the grace given at Baptism.

3. The physical sign of the sacrament is anointing with a perfumed oil consecrated by the bishop. This oil is called:
   (a) balsam
   (b) sanctum
   (c) chrism

4. The bishop consecrates the sacred oil of Confirmation at this liturgy each year:
   (a) Holy Thursday
   (b) Easter Vigil
   (c) Pentecost

5. For the essential rite of the sacrament—that is, the basic and necessary elements of the sacrament—the anointing with oil is accompanied by which other action?
   (a) laying on of the hands
   (b) reception of Holy Eucharist
   (c) sign of peace

6. The essential words spoken by the bishop in the administration of the sacrament are:
   (a) "Go forth and be his witnesses"
   (b) "You are now confirmed"
   (c) "Be sealed with the Gift of the Holy Spirit"

7. The bishop is the ordinary minister of this sacrament primarily because:
   (a) he is a successor to the apostles, who bore witness to Christ
   (b) it is a longstanding traditional practice
   (c) only he is permitted to use the sacred oil

8. Upon receiving the sacrament, the confirmand receives an indelible spiritual mark, the seal of the Holy Spirit, which means:
   (a) he will never commit a mortal sin
   (b) he has received a special power from Christ to be his witness
   (c) his education in the faith is completed

9. Those eligible to receive the sacrament are:
   (a) every baptized person not yet confirmed
   (b) baptized persons who have reached the age of reason
   (c) young adults, whether baptized or not

10. Before receiving Confirmation, one must receive the Sacrament of Penance:
    (a) at least once
    (b) if he has committed a mortal sin
    (c) within one month prior to being confirmed

Anointing with Oil

NAME _____

The use of oils has a long symbolic tradition, dating to its practical and ritual uses in ancient cultures. The various meanings associated with anointing are integrated into the sacraments of the Church, four in particular: Baptism, Confirmation, Holy Orders, and Anointing of the Sick.

In this activity, you are given some of the physical and symbolic qualities of oil and anointing. For each one, look up and copy the Scripture verse or verses given, then write the name of the sacraments for which the meaning is applicable.

1. Sign of abundance and joy

Psalm 23:5 _____

_____

Sacrament(s) _____

2. Sign of cleansing

Judith 10:1–3 _____

_____

Sacrament(s) _____

3. Sign of healing

Luke 10:34 _____

_____

Sacrament(s) _____

_____

4. Sign of strength

1 Samuel 10:1 _____

_____

Sacrament(s) _____

_____

5. Sign of beauty (perfumed oil)

2 Corinthians 2:15 _____

_____

Sacrament(s) _____

_____

6. Sign of consecration

Exodus 30:30 _____

_____

Sacrament(s) _____

_____

100 Activities Based on the Catechism of the Catholic Church
© 2013 Ignatius Press

A Scriptural Examination of Conscience

Before you receive the Sacrament of Penance, or Reconciliation, you think about your sins. How have your choices—your thoughts and actions— lived up to your call from Christ? How have you kept God's commandments? How have you loved God and neighbor?

This process is an examination of conscience. It helps us to identify sins and sinful habits that we can confess to the priest in order to receive penance and forgiveness. We can even do a brief examination daily, so we can be aware of our weaknesses and turn to God for grace and pardon.

Many guides and questionnaires have been written to help us in this examination. Some are based on the Ten Commandments, others on Jesus' two great commandments or the Beatitudes. The rite of the sacrament indicates that whatever form it takes, our examination of conscience should be made "in the light of the Word of God".

In this exercise, you will make your own guide for an examination of conscience based on some key Scriptures. Read each verse, and think about how it applies to someone your age. Then write one or more questions based on the passage to help someone like yourself make a good examination. An example is given below.

(**Hint:** *Some sins are things we do that we should not do; others are things we do not do that we should do.*)

Matthew 5:22 (on anger)
> *Have I gotten angry with my parents, my brothers or sisters, or friends? Have I used harsh language or profanity? Have I said or done anything hurtful out of anger?*

Matthew 5:28 (on lust)

_____

_____

Matthew 5:43–48 (on love of enemies)

_____

_____

Matthew 6:6 (on prayer)

_____

Matthew 6:14–15 (on forgiveness)

_____

Matthew 6:24 and 2 Timothy 6:9 (on money)

_____

Matthew 7:1–5 (on judging)

_____

Romans 12:16 (on pride)

_____

Romans 13:1–7 (on obedience to authority)

_____

1 Corinthians 13:4–6 (on love)

_____

Ephesians 4:25 (on truth)

_____

Ephesians 4:28 (on stealing)

_____

Ephesians 5:3–4 (on right speech)

_____

Ephesians 6:1–3 (on obeying parents)

_____

The Sacrament of Matrimony

NAME

Fill in the blanks from the word bank to complete these statements based on the *Catechism*.

| word | love | grace | consent | dissolved |
| life | Christ | faithful | children | trial marriage |

1. God, who created man out of love, also calls him to _____—the fundamental and innate vocation of every human being.

2. The _____ by which the spouses mutually give and receive one another is sealed by God himself.

3. Therefore the marriage bond between baptized persons can never be _____.

4. The covenant that spouses have freely entered into entails _____ love.

5. Fidelity in marriage means keeping one's given _____.

6. A _____ _____ is not a total and definitive gift of a man and a woman to one another.

7. The _____ proper to the Sacrament of Marriage works to perfect the couple's love.

8. _____ is the source of this grace.

9. _____ are the supreme gift of marriage and contribute greatly to the good of the parents themselves.

10. The fundamental task of marriage and family is to be at the service of _____.

The Seven Primary Virtues

NAME

Human beings are made in the image and likeness of God. As explained in the *Catechism of the Catholic Church*, this means two things: We find happiness in goodness, and we have a free will to choose this happiness. The original sin of Adam and Eve has injured our human nature to make it easy and inviting to do the evil that will bring us sorrow instead of the good that will bring us joy. However, our free response to the grace of the Holy Spirit and the practice of the moral life helps us to achieve the fulfillment for which we are made.

To find happiness in goodness, we need virtues, which is another way of saying that we need to form habits of being and doing good. There are seven primary virtues and they are defined below.

The first three virtues are theological, that is they come from and are directed toward God.

Faith: The virtue by which we believe in God and all he has said and revealed.
—CCC 1814

Hope: The virtue by which we long for heaven and trust in God's help to attain it.
—CCC 1817

Charity: The highest of all virtues, by which we love God and love our neighbor.
—CCC 1822

The four cardinal virtues are those that are directed to our own good and that of others. The word "cardinal" means "hinge", and all of our good actions depend upon these virtues.

Prudence: The knowledge of what is to be done and what is to be avoided in each situation.
—CCC 1806

Justice: The determination to give what we owe to God and our neighbor.
—CCC 1807

Fortitude: The strength to do what we should even in the face of difficulties.
—CCC 1808

Temperance: The self-control to moderate our desire for pleasure, whether that comes from food, drink, sleep, entertainment, etc.
—CCC 1809

On the next page are two activities to help you learn these virtues.

The Seven Primary Virtues, cont'd

NAME _____

Activity A

Acquiring a virtue, like acquiring any good habit, takes practice. Even though we are given the theological virtues of faith, hope, and charity at our Baptism, we need to practice these virtues so that they grow strong. The Church gives us three disciplines to help us grow in these virtues: prayer, fasting and almsgiving. Discuss as a class and answer the questions below.

1. Prayer is conversation with God. How does talking with God strengthen our faith in him?

   _____

   _____

   _____

   _____

2. When we fast from food or abstain from something we would like to have or do, we feel weak in the face of our desires. We can cave in, or we can turn to God for strength. How does relying on God build up our hope in him?

   _____

   _____

   _____

   _____

3. When we give alms, we give time, money, material goods, or personal service to those in need. How does doing such things increase our love for others?

   _____

   _____

   _____

   _____

100 Activities Based on the Catechism of the Catholic Church
© 2013 Ignatius Press

The Seven Primary Virtues, cont'd

NAME

Activity B

Prudence — Justice — Fortitude — Temperance

These four virtues are needed to do good actions. For each action described below, write the first letter of the virtue that is needed to do it. Although all the virtues work together, choose the one that fits the best.

1. _____ Even though you would like to have another one, you decline a second brownie.

2. _____ You feel like quitting, but you finish a difficult math problem.

3. _____ The cashier neglected to charge for a shirt, and you go back to pay for it.

4. _____ You listen carefully to your father's instructions before using the lawn mower.

5. _____ After losing your friend's DVD, you buy her another one.

6. _____ You can see your classmate's test sheet, but you refuse to look at his answers.

7. _____ Even though you would rather go home, you go to your team's workout after school.

8. _____ Knowing you have lots of homework, you decide to do the hardest subject first.

9. _____ You stop yourself from starting to play another video game.

10. _____ You save some of your babysitting money to buy something special later.

11. _____ A bit of gossip is on the tip of your tongue, and you stop yourself from blurting it out.

12. _____ You plan your weekend ahead of time so that you will fit in everything you wish to do.

13. _____ You get out of bed when the alarm goes off, even though you are comfortable.

14. _____ While doing the dishes, you wash out the last pan you feel like leaving in the sink.

15. _____ You go to Mass on Sunday because God deserves your thanks and praise.

16. _____ The party is going in a bad direction, and you call your parents to pick you up.

You and Society

You probably hear adults discussing social issues or talking about the good or bad aspects of our contemporary society. What exactly is society? Is it politics? Is it the media, music, and other parts of popular culture? Do only adults participate? Is it something to which you belong and can make a contribution?

A society is an organized group of individuals who come together for a common purpose that is beyond any one of those individuals. A society can be as small and intimate as a family, or as large and complex as the state or country of which they are citizens.

Since the fall of Adam, original sin has created the potential for harm to individuals through the societies in which they live. Some societies, for example, fail to regard the dignity of each individual person. Through Christ, however, we are redeemed, and in him we can work toward the redemption of the societies in which we live.

Your family, your school, your community, and your sports teams and other clubs are some of the societies to which you belong, and all share some common features. For example, all of them have some form of **authority**, a person or people who govern the society and take responsibility for its well-being. Authority is legitimate when it is moral and seeks the good of all. Societies also have a common mission, or **purpose**, which holds them together and focuses the efforts of individuals. Each person has a **duty** to perform within the communities to which he belongs. Finally, everyone has different **talents** and strengths to contribute to the communities to which he belongs, and those are in turn developed within those communities.

- -

On the next page of this activity, describe five of the societies to which you belong. For each society, write its name, authority, and purpose, and then your own duties toward each and the talents you bring to each.

100 Activities Based on the Catechism of the Catholic Church
© 2013 Ignatius Press

You and Society

NAME

1. **Family**
   Name:
   Authority:
   Purpose:
   My personal duty:
   My talents:

2. **School**
   Name:
   Authority:
   Purpose:
   My personal duty:
   My talents:

3. **Local community**
   Name:
   Authority:
   Purpose:
   My personal duty:
   My talents:

4. **Club or team (A)**
   Name:
   Authority:
   Purpose:
   My personal duty:
   My talents:

5. **Club or team (B)**
   Name:
   Authority:
   Purpose:
   My personal duty:
   My talents:

Freedom and Morality

NAME

Made in the image of God, man has a free will. That is, he can control his own thoughts and actions. Because of this innate freedom, man's actions can be morally judged as good or evil. Solve this crossword puzzle, using the clues that explore the various concepts of freedom and morality.

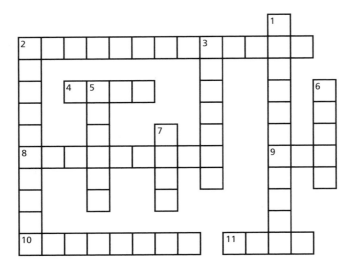

ACROSS

2. The conditions relevant to an act, which affect the moral evaluation of that act. (One of three sources of morality of human acts.)
4. One general guideline of morality is that a person may not do evil even if _____ may result from it.
8. A second source of morality, which refers to the purpose in mind of the one committing the act. Synonyms: plan, purpose.
9. To go against the judgment of one's conscience—or what one knows or believes is right—is to _____.
10. Synonym for "feelings" or "passions". They are not moral in and of themselves but can contribute to a good or bad action.
11. Christ has set us _____ from the slavery of sin.

DOWN

1. Because we have free will, we are _____ for our actions.
2. The inner voice that helps a person decide if an act is right or wrong.
3. Choices a person makes that can be judged as good or evil are called moral _____.
5. The third source of morality. It is a good toward which the will directs itself, or the thing chosen. Synonymous with "thing".
6. The ends do not justify the _____.
7. A virtue is a habitual and _____ disposition to do good. Synonyms: strong, unyielding.

100 Activities Based on the Catechism of the Catholic Church
© 2013 Ignatius Press

The Precepts of the Church

TEACHER-DIRECTED ACTIVITY

Say: The Ten Commandments, given by God to Moses on Mount Sinai, are described in the *Catechism* as a "path of life" for the Hebrew people and a proclamation of God's law.

Jesus summarized the Ten Commandments into two great commandments: "Love the Lord your God with all your heart, and with all your soul, and with all your mind . . . and . . . You shall love your neighbor as yourself" (Matthew 22:37).

With these commandments as the "gold standard" for moral living, the *Catechism* also teaches us about five positive laws established by the Catholic Church. They are positive because they are written as things we must do, rather than things we must not do.

The precepts are not a high bar, but a low bar—they are the minimum to help us to grow in faith and a holy life.

The Precepts of the Church

1. You shall attend Mass on Sundays and on holy days of obligation and rest from servile labor.
2. You shall confess your sins at least once a year.
3. You shall receive the sacrament of the Eucharist at least during the Easter season.
4. You shall observe the days of fasting and abstinence established by the Church.
5. You shall help to provide for the needs of the Church.

(*Option:* Write these on the board, or have students write them on paper.)

Activity A: A "Precept Cheer"

Say: Here is a shorthand for the five precepts:

1. Sunday Mass
2. Confess Yearly
3. Eucharist at Easter
4. Fast and Abstain
5. Provide for the Church

Let's practice them as if we were cheering during a football game.

Directions: Divide the class into two sides. One side will shout, "Church Precepts", and the other will respond, "Sunday Mass"; the first side will shout, "Confess Yearly", and the other will respond, "Eucharist at Easter", and so on down the list. Go through a couple of rounds, alternating the team that begins. Next, the teacher can call on individual students to call them out in order, one after another (Student 1 says, "Sunday Mass"; Student 2, "Confess Yearly", etc.)

The Precepts of the Church

NAME

Activity B: A "Precept Paragraph"

It's good to know the precepts by heart, but more important to know the heart of the precepts. Why should we follow them? Consider that if we were to fall out of the practice of Sunday Mass attendance, over time we likely would find our faith growing weak. If parishioners took the attitude that a gift in the offering is an optional donation rather than a necessity, they might find their parish unable to pay its bills to run the church.

Choose one precept from Activity A and write a paragraph explaining its importance.

_____

_____

_____

_____

_____

_____

_____

_____

_____

_____

The First Commandment

NAME

The first of the Ten Commandments begins with a statement of God's love for us: **"I am the Lord your God, who brought you out of the land of Egypt, out of the house of bondage."** It then continues with the call for us to love God in return: **"You shall have no other gods before me"** (Exodus 20:2–3).

To seek God is a sure way to find him, and to worship and love him is the path to happiness in this life and in eternity. Yet the human heart can be pulled in the wrong direction, through sins against this commandment, including superstition and irreligion, and through false beliefs of atheism and agnosticism.

Activity A

Circle the letter of the correct answer to these five statements or questions.
(See *Catechism*, paragraphs 2111–2128).

1. A **superstition** is a belief that certain prayers or actions have power that belongs to God. An example of *superstition* is:
   A. Burying a statue of St. Joseph in the yard, believing this action alone has the power to sell a house.
   B. Placing a statue of Mary on a shelf as a reminder of her holiness and motherly love.

2. **Idolatry** is to worship many gods or to worship as God what is not God. It can be *idolatry* to:
   C. Attend the concert of a favorite singer instead of going to Mass.
   D. Revere the saints as examples of God's transforming love.

3. To commit **sacrilege** is to disrespect sacraments, persons, things, or places that are consecrated to God. An example of *sacrilege* is:
   E. To write a respectful letter of complaint to your pastor.
   F. To send text messages during Mass instead of paying attention to the liturgy.

4. **Atheism**, which is the rejection of God or the denial that God exists, is a major problem in the world today. How can we as believers address this problem?
   G. Warn atheists that they are evil and selfish
   H. Mind our own business and wait for people to come to faith
   I. Grow in our faith, teach the faith truthfully to others, and live a good moral life.

5. There is another growing problem in the world, of those who do not reject God but declare that it is impossible to prove or disprove his existence. This belief is known as:
   J. Agnosticism
   K. Polytheism

The First Commandment

Activity B

Referring to Activity A, follow the path through the letters of the correct answers, in order, to get through the maze.

START

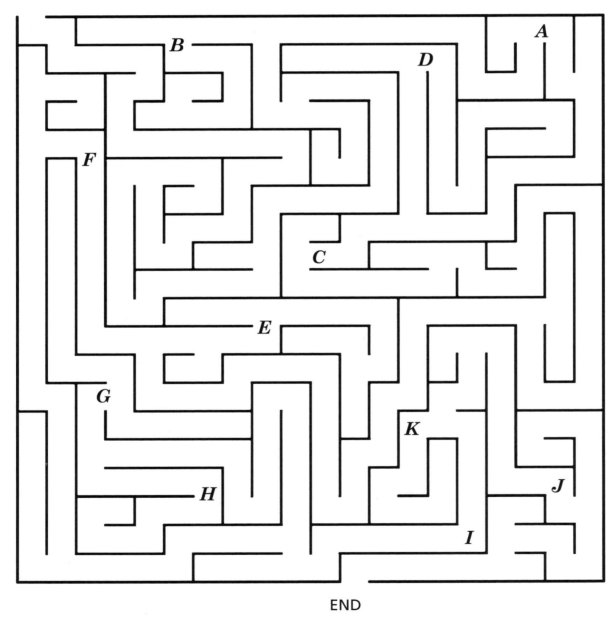

END

100 Activities Based on the Catechism of the Catholic Church
© 2013 Ignatius Press

The Gospel of Life

NAME

In 1995, Pope John Paul II addressed the bishops, the universal Church, and "all people of good will" with the powerful encyclical letter *Evangelium vitae*, or *The Gospel of Life*. In this challenging statement, which quotes from the *Catechism of the Catholic Church* and reaffirms its teaching, Pope John Paul II described the current threats to human life and called for a new culture of life based on God's holy law.

Read these nine selected passages from *The Gospel of Life*. On a separate sheet of paper, write a brief answer to the nine questions.

1. "Humanity today offers us a truly alarming spectacle, if we consider not only how extensively attacks on life are spreading, but also their unheard-of numerical proportion, and the fact that they receive widespread and powerful support from a broad consensus on the part of society, from widespread legal approval and the involvement of certain sectors of health-care personnel" (chapter 1, no. 17).

   —*Give an example of attacks on human life.*

2. Pope John Paul II writes that the loss of a sense of God leads to practical materialism: "The values of being are replaced by those of having. The only goal which counts is the pursuit of one's own material well-being" (chapter 1, no. 23).

   —*In what ways have you seen this attitude of materialism in our culture?*

3. "Through the words, the actions and the very person of Jesus, man is given the possibility of 'knowing' the complete truth concerning the value of human life" (chapter 2, no. 29).

   —*Give two or more examples from the life of Christ in which he illuminated the value of human life.*

4. Upholding the principle stated in the *Catechism* that bloodless means should be used to defend human lives whenever such means are sufficient to protect public order and the safety of persons, Pope John Paul II says this about the death penalty: "The nature of and extent of the punishment must be carefully evaluated and decided upon, and ought not go to the extreme of executing the offender except in cases of absolute necessity: in other words, when it would not be possible otherwise to defend society. Today, however, as a result of steady improvements in the organization of the penal system, such cases are very rare, if not practically non-existent" (chapter 3, no. 56).

   —*What is the Holy Father saying about the death penalty?*

5. "I confirm that the direct and voluntary killing of an innocent human being is always gravely immoral. This doctrine, based upon that unwritten law which man, in the light of reason, finds in his own heart (cf. Rom. 2:14–15), is reaffirmed by Sacred Scripture, transmitted by the Tradition of the Church and taught by the ordinary and universal Magisterium" (chapter 3, no. 57).

   —*List the four means by which we can be certain of the truth of this doctrine.*

Continued next page

The Gospel of Life, cont'd

6. "Among all the crimes which can be committed against life, procured abortion has characteristics making it particularly serious and deplorable. The Second Vatican Council defines abortion, together with infanticide, as an 'unspeakable crime'" (chapter 3, no. 58).

—*What makes abortion so morally evil as to be called "unspeakable"?*

7. "When the prevailing tendency is to value life only to the extent that it brings pleasure and well-being, suffering seems like an unbearable setback, something from which one must be freed at all costs. Death is considered 'senseless' if it suddenly interrupts a life still open to a future of new and interesting experiences. But it becomes a 'rightful liberation' once life is held to be no longer meaningful because it is filled with pain and inexorably doomed to even greater suffering" (chapter 3, no. 64).

—*What value does a Christian find in suffering?*

8. "For a correct moral judgment on euthanasia, in the first place a clear definition is required. Euthanasia in the strict sense is understood to be an action or omission which of itself and by intention causes death, with the purpose of eliminating all suffering" (chapter 3, no. 65).

—*Which of the following are **not** about euthanasia?*

A. "To concur with the intention of another person to commit suicide and to help in carrying it out through so-called 'assisted suicide' . . ." (chapter 3, no. 66).

B. ". . . 'methods of palliative care,' which seek to make suffering more bearable in the final stages of illness . . . even when the result is decreased consciousness and a shortening of life, 'if no other means exist . . .'" to relieve pain (chapter 3, no. 65).

C. The decision to forego medical treatments "which no longer correspond to the real situation of the patient, either because they are by now disproportionate to any expected results or because they impose an excessive burden on the patient and his family . . . when death is clearly imminent and inevitable . . ." (chapter 3, no. 65).

D. ". . . when certain people, such as physicians or legislators, arrogate to themselves the power to decide who ought to live and who ought to die" (chapter 3, no. 66).

9. ". . . the *Gospel of Life* is to be celebrated above all in daily living, which should be filled with self-giving love for others" (chapter 4, no. 86).

—*What are some ways a person your age can help bring about a "culture of life"?*

100 Activities Based on the Catechism of the Catholic Church
© 2013 Ignatius Press

The Seventh Commandment

NAME

The Seventh Commandment teaches us in four simple words: ***"You shall not steal."*** The *Catechism of the Catholic Church* explains how these words point to many truths about the right use of this world's goods, in the context of the love of God and neighbor. The goods of creation were given as an original gift to all mankind. But in order to promote the common good, individuals also have a right to private property, which is to be used in moderation, to be shared with those in need, and not to be taken away by individuals or governments.

Activity A

Carefully read the *Catechism*, paragraphs 2401 to 2463. Then match the term on the left with the phrase on the right.

Matching phrase

Term

_____ A. Seventh Commandment

_____ B. Temperance

_____ C. Slavery

_____ D. Just wage

_____ E. Aid to the poor

_____ F. Gambling

_____ G. Duty to animals

_____ H. Private property ownership

_____ I. Work

1. Kindness, but not the affection due only to persons

2. Is wrong if it deprives a person of the means to provide for oneself or one's family

3. Is a duty inscribed in man's nature

4. A work of justice and sign of fraternal love that pleases God

5. Forbids unjustly taking or keeping the goods of one's neighbor

6. The virtue that moderates attachment to this world's goods

7. A right and also a duty that binds one to a form of stewardship to benefit one's own family first, and then others

8. Legitimate fruit of work that may not be withheld

9. Sins against the dignity and rights of persons by reducing them by violence to a source of profit

The Seventh Commandment

NAME

Activity B

After completing Activity A, write in the numbers that match the grey letters in the Sudoku puzzle. Then complete the puzzle. (*Note:* each column, row, and 9-square block contains all the numbers from 1 to 9 with no repeating.)

	9		4	A	7		8	
5		7	1	B	8	9		2
	8			2	C		1	
2	1	D					3	6
	E	3				8		
9	6		F				7	1
	5	G		3			9	
8		6	9	H	1	3		4
I	7		5		2		6	

100 Activities Based on the Catechism of the Catholic Church
© 2013 Ignatius Press

The Eighth Commandment

TEACHER-DIRECTED ACTIVITY

Purpose: to encourage students in the right use of speech in building up one another in Christ.

Hint: This activity is better suited for the second semester, when students are better acquainted. It will take more than one class period.

Directions

Set up in front of the classroom one chair facing the class and, next to that, a desk with chair, also facing the class. At the desk place some notebook paper and a pen.

Ask: Who can tell me what the Eighth Commandment says? [*Elicit the full response: You shall not bear false witness against your neighbor. If the students are a little rusty, you may want to take a few minutes to review the Ten Commandments with them, or to schedule a review at your next opportunity.*] What does it mean to bear false witness? [*To tell a lie, to conceal the truth, and so on.*] We break this commandment every time we commit an offense against truth. The *Catechism of the Catholic Church* actually lists several ways we can break this commandment, ways that we do not always think of.

For example, it is wrong to commit perjury, that is, to break an oath to tell the truth before a judge or jury in a court of law. What harm could come from perjury? [*Guilty person might go free, or innocent person might be found guilty.*]

How about something a little more commonplace. Have you ever heard the word "detraction"? That means talking about someone's faults to another person who didn't know of those faults. What harm can come from that? [*Hurts person's reputation, weakens trust between speaker and listener, and so on.*]

How about "rash judgment"? That means you believe without evidence something bad about another person. Why might this be wrong? [*We are accountable to God for our thoughts; Jesus told us not to judge others, for we will be judged in the same way as we have judged others.*]

Did you know that boasting, or bragging, also breaks the Eighth Commandment? What does it mean to boast? [*To talk about oneself or one's accomplishments in a proud or vain way.*] Why is that an offense against truth? [*We are all here by the grace of God and are not self-sufficient.*]

Does it seem pretty easy to break the Eighth Commandment? For some people, it can be a real struggle not to do so. Listen to what Saint James said in his letter to the Church: "No human being can tame the tongue—a restless evil, full of deadly poison. With it we bless the Lord and Father, and with it we curse men who are made in the likeness of God." Sad, but true. Yet, James is not without hope, for he goes on to say "this need not be so" (James 3:8–10). As with any struggle against sin, we don't give up, we engage in battle, using the spiritual weapons of the sacraments, prayer, spiritual reading, and spending time with mature Christians.

Now, if to break the Eighth Commandment means to bear false witness, to obey the Eighth Commandment must mean to bear *true* witness. We're going to play a game that will give us the chance to do that.

Choose two students, one to be the "candidate" and the other to be the "interviewer". The candidate is to sit in the chair facing the class, and the interviewer will sit in the chair at the desk. The first interviewer should be someone who is comfortable talking in front of the class.

Continued

The Eighth Commandment, cont'd

Say: "Jane" is our first candidate. She is running for the Image of God award. "Joe" is her interviewer. Everyone will be needed to take part in this game, and everyone will have a turn up here in front.

Joe is going to begin this game by writing down the nicest thing he can think of about Jane to indicate why she should be selected for the Image of God award. We'll give him a minute or two. His reason could be a good deed she has done for him or someone else, something about her personality or her character, or whatever it is that he thinks makes her an outstanding image of God. [*When Joe is finished writing, have him read what he wrote to the class.*] Now Joe is ready to do some interviews. He wants to know what everyone else can say about Jane in favor of her selection as Image of God. The judges like to hear different kinds of statements, so try to say something that has not already been mentioned. Joe will write them all down. All right, raise your hands as you think of something, and Joe will call on you.

Proceed as described. Everyone should participate—after it gets going, this should continue fairly easily, as students will rise to the occasion of praising another.

Say: Now, Joe, you may give this list to Jane. It is hers to keep. I think we can all agree that Jane should win the award! [*Lead applause.*] Now, Jane, it is your turn to be the interviewer, and I would like you to call on the next candidate.

Game proceeds as before. Continue to play until the end of the period, and continue in as many class periods as needed—it may take two or three—until everyone has had a turn as a candidate. It is vital that everyone has a turn, so be sure you have allowed enough time in your schedule. If desirable, this may be done as a "last 10 minutes of class" activity for as many days as there are students.

After everyone has had a chance to receive praise, pass out copies of Activity 96. Ask students to write their answers to the questions in class or at home. Call on various students to share their answers with the class. Allow time for discussion.

Option 1

Teacher can be the interviewer, if class lacks the maturity to conduct this activity.

Option 2

Rather than having the interviewer call on students and record their comments, some time can be given for all the students to write their statements, simultaneously and anonymously, after which the teacher can collect them and selectively read them aloud. Students should be given all positive comments to keep.

The Eighth Commandment

NAME

You have received feedback from your classmates about which qualities you possess that reflect the image of God. Write down your answers to the following questions and discuss them as a class.

1. How did it feel to receive positive comments from your classmates?

_____

_____

2. How would you have felt if the comments had been critical or negative?

_____

_____

3. Why is it important to *receive* sincere praise from others?

_____

_____

4. Why is it important to *give* sincere praise to others? And what should be your motive for doing so?

_____

_____

5. What is flattery, why is it given, and why is it against the Eighth Commandment?

_____

_____

_____

6. Is it ever right or correct to give constructive criticism? When? And what should be the motive or reason for doing so?

_____

_____

_____

Social Media and the Gospel

NAME

The *Catechism of the Catholic Church* teaches that the communications media serve an important role in spreading information as well as shaping the formation of individuals and culture. The media should serve the common good by providing information based on truth, freedom, justice, and building community, and should avoid defaming others or invading their privacy. The practice of tyrannical governments to misuse media to spread falsehoods, intimidate persons, or suppress free thought is to be condemned.

Social media are a more recent phenomenon, in which private individuals can disseminate ideas and images instantly to a wide audience through the Internet. Just as those working in the mass media need to exercise moral judgment, so too should private individuals take care to be truthful, charitable, prudent, and modest in their Internet and phone communications. As consumers of media, we need to practice moderation in our use of the Internet, think critically about what we read and see online, and strictly avoid impure images and degrading messages.

In 2012, Pope Benedict XVI became the first pope to Tweet, and in so doing followed the tradition of popes before him to address the world using the media available to them: In 1931, Pope Pius XI made the first papal radio broadcast; in 1946, Pope Pius XII made the first papal television appearance; and in 2001, Pope John Paul II became the first pope to send an email.

While Pope Benedict acknowledged the human desire for community that is at the heart of social media, in his message for the 2011 celebration of World Communications Day he also cautioned: "Entering cyberspace can be a sign of an authentic search for personal encounters with others, provided that attention is paid to avoiding dangers such as enclosing oneself in a sort of parallel existence, or excessive exposure to the virtual world. In the search for sharing, for 'friends', there is the challenge to be authentic and faithful, and not give in to the illusion of constructing an artificial public profile for oneself."

Individuals can use online media as new means to spread the faith, while recognizing that these cannot replace actual, personal encounters. Said Pope Benedict: "Even when it is proclaimed in the virtual space of the Web, the gospel demands to be incarnated in the real world and linked to the real faces of our brothers and sisters."

*   *   *

Just for fun, write out some Tweets (with 140 characters or fewer) to share the gospel.

> **Example:** Jesus came and changed everything. Go to a nearby Catholic Church and find out how!

_____

_____

_____

The Ninth Commandment

Our world today is very confused about the **gift of the human person** and how we are to love one another through our bodies. The *Catechism of the Catholic Church* teaches us the meaning of the Ninth Commandment and how we can rely on God's grace to obey it and, in so doing, find both happiness and holiness.

Read the *Catechism*, paragraphs 2514 to 2533, and then match each term in the left column with the corresponding phrase in the right column.

Term	*Matching phrase*
_____ 1. Ninth Commandment	**A.** Both body and spirit
_____ 2. Purity of heart	**B.** Disordered desires
_____ 3. Modesty	**C.** Should be guided by modesty
_____ 4. Purity of intention	**D.** Wanting a person for physical pleasure
_____ 5. Adultery of the heart	**E.** Seeking to find and fulfill God's will
_____ 6. Good news of Christ	**F.** Incorrect idea of purity
_____ 7. A human person	**G.** You shall not covet your neighbor's wife
_____ 8. Concupiscence	**H.** Allows us the vision of God
_____ 9. Choice of clothing	**I.** Renews the life and culture of man
_____ 10. Lust	**J.** Protects the heart and dignity of persons
_____ 11. Despising the gift of one's body	**K.** Looking at another with lust

Understanding the Our Father

NAME _____

It has been called "the most perfect of prayers" (Saint Thomas Aquinas), the sum of all the prayers in Scripture (Saint Augustine), and the "summary of the whole gospel" (Church Father Tertullian). The Our Father, also known as the Lord's Prayer because it was given to us by Jesus, holds a unique and honorable place in the life of the Church. We find the Lord's Prayer in the Sunday Mass, in the Liturgy of the Hours, and in the rites of Baptism and Confirmation.

For all its frequent use and familiarity, the Our Father was never intended by our Lord to be a mere recitation. When you pray, you should direct your mind and heart to God so that "you remain in me and my words remain in you" (Jn 15:7).

To increase your understanding of the Our Father, look up the following Bible verses. On a separate sheet of paper, answer the questions.

Our Father   —*Galatians 3:26, 4:6*

1. Why do we call the God of the universe our Father?

2. If God is our Father, who are we to each other?

who art in heaven   —*Revelation 7:9–17*

3. Using Saint John's vision as a guide, how do you imagine heaven?

hallowed be thy name   —*John 12:27, 28*

4. This part of the Our Father is the first of seven petitions, or prayerful requests, that make up the rest of the Lord's Prayer. If we understand this phrase not as praise but as a petition, what are we asking of God?

Thy kingdom come   —*Matthew 25:31–34*

5. When we pray this petition, what are we asking for?

Thy will be done on earth as it is in heaven   —*John 13:34*

6. What is God's will?

Give us this day our daily bread   —*John 6:5–14, 22–27*

7. God satisfies what two types of hunger?

8. What is the "food which endures to eternal life" that Jesus feeds us?

9. This petition also implies responsibilities for Christians. What are they?

and forgive us our trespasses as we forgive those who trespass against us   —*Matthew 18:23–35*

10. This petition is remarkable in that it does not stand alone but comes with a condition, linked by the word "as". Restate the entire petition in your own words.

11. The divine forgiveness Jesus asks of us would be impossible for us to give on our own strength. Who dwells within us to enable us to forgive one another as God has forgiven us?

and lead us not into temptation   —*1 Corinthians 10:13*

12. How does God help us in time of temptation?

but deliver us from evil.   —*John 17:15*

13. In this petition, from whom do we ask to be delivered?

The Priestly Prayer of Jesus (John 17)

NAME

The last of Jesus' discourses to his disciples, as written by the evangelist and apostle John (Jn 17), is a prayer, the longest prayer in the Gospels. Called the "prayer of Jesus", or the "prayer of the hour of Jesus", this appeal to his Father unveils the plan of salvation from the beginning of the world to Christ's glory in heaven.

Since the sixteenth century, this chapter has been called the "priestly prayer" of Jesus, who intercedes for his followers as he prepares for his consecration as high priest and as sacrifice. Also in this prayer we find echoes of the Our Father, whose petitions it fulfills.

*   *   *

Read the prayer in your Bibles. Then answer the questions.

1. In which verse does Jesus mention his "hour"? What is his hour?

    _____

    _____

2. In which verse does Jesus begin to pray for us, his present-day disciples?

    _____

3. Which of Jesus' disciples was "lost", as mentioned in verse 12?

    _____

Match the verse from Jesus' prayer on the left with the petition from the Our Father that it fulfills on the right.

_____ 4. Verses 22–24   **A.** "hallowed be thy name"

_____ 5. Verse 15   **B.** "thy kingdom come"

_____ 6. Verses 4 and 26   **C.** "thy will be done"

_____ 7. Verse 6   **D.** "but deliver us from evil"

Fifteen Minutes with God

TEACHER-DIRECTED ACTIVITY

Materials: Bibles, copies of "Scriptures and Prayer Steps" (see next page), prayer journals (five sheets notebook paper stapled, or three sheets blank paper folded in half and stapled in center like a book).

Purpose: to encourage in students the practice of daily prayer and to introduce them to meditation on the Scriptures as a way to communion with God.

Directions

Distribute Bibles, prayer guidelines (see next page), and blank paper for prayer journals to students.

Say: Let's pretend the president of the United States is coming to town, and he wants to put his finger on the pulse of America, so to speak. He wants to talk to some ordinary citizens to learn what their concerns are, their opinions about current issues, and so on. Your family has been randomly chosen for the visit. In fact, he will be coming over to your house tomorrow, and he wants to have 15 minutes with you, personally, to talk to you about some of his programs and to listen to your hopes and fears about the country. You may even be on the network news for a minute or two.

What would you do to get ready? [*Read recent newspapers, get a haircut, help clean the house, tell your friends, and so forth.*] Now, you're a busy person. You might have to miss a ball practice or music lesson for this. Would you still do it? [*Of course!*] Why? [*He's the president, chance of a lifetime, an honor, and so forth.*]

What if, by some strange turn of events, the president now wants you as a youth adviser, and he wants to be able to talk with you by phone every day, for about fifteen minutes. That's a lot of time out of your life. Would

you do it, even if it meant getting up earlier in the morning, or taking some personal time after school? [*Yes.*] Why? [*Great opportunity, lot of influence, and so on.*]

The fact is, there is someone more important, more powerful, and more interested in you than the president, who would like to meet with you every day. That Person is God himself. He wants us to be in touch with him all through the day, but it is hard to do that unless we deliberately set aside a certain time to give him our full attention.

Probably you already have some kind of prayer practice—maybe you say certain prayers at night before sleeping or in the morning to give your day to God. You pray at Mass, and I know you pray before tests! Most of us need help and encouragement to grow in prayer. So, for the next week, I want us all to commit to a fifteen-minute appointment with God for five days between now and when we meet next. [*For classes that meet daily, this can be done in any five- to seven-day period.*] Does fifteen minutes sound like a long time to pray? One five-decade Rosary prayed devoutly takes about that long.

Rather than our formal prayers, we will try meditation, specifically, meditation on the Scriptures. You might have heard of meditation in the context of Eastern religions, but actually there is a long tradition of Christian meditation. On the sheet I've given you are Scriptures for each day and a guideline for your meditation prayer. You also have some blank paper in which to make a prayer journal. Your journal is private. At the end of the week, we'll discuss how our prayer appointments went and what we learned.

Fifteen Minutes with God: Scriptures and Prayer Steps

> Day One: Psalm 95:1–7

> Day Two: Proverbs 3:13–35

> Day Three: Ephesians 3:14–21

> Day Four: Psalm 139:1–18

> Day Five: Luke 15:11–32

STEP 1
Choose a time and place in which you can have privacy and quiet and can be somewhat alert. Try getting up 15 minutes earlier in the morning.

STEP 2
Invite the Holy Spirit to inspire you as you read and guide you in your prayer.

STEP 3
Read the Scripture passage all the way through, then go back and read the verses more slowly.

STEP 4
Stop at any verse or phrase that seems to jump out or have special meaning.

STEP 5
Listen to God speak in that verse, or in the whole passage.

STEP 6
Try to put yourself in the passage, making the scriptural prayer your own, or envisioning yourself in the scene. Use your imagination to see, hear, or touch what the words describe.

STEP 7
Talk to God about what you've read. There's no need to be formal; be yourself. Write your thoughts, responses, feelings, or prayers in your prayer journal. If it helps you, start the page with "Dear God" or "Dear Jesus".

STEP 8
Be open to any or all of the five forms of prayer: adoration, praise, thanksgiving, petition, and intercession.

STEP 9
Don't worry if you get distracted; it is common. Just turn your attention back to the Lord.

Fifteen Minutes with God: Class Discussion

TEACHER-DIRECTED ACTIVITY

Note: If you meet for class daily, you should remind your students to be keeping their appointments each day. Set an example by keeping yours!

> ### Questions for class discussion
> How did your appointments go?
>
> What makes prayer difficult?
>
> What makes prayer rewarding?
>
> Where and when do you like to pray best?
>
> What would help you to continue to pray daily?

Be open to helping students find books or other aids about prayer; many such resources exist. Also, you might suggest that students continue their 15 minutes by prayerfully reading through the Gospels, one chapter a day.

Answer Keys

Activity 1, page 7

1. leaf
2. cat
3. stars
4. fish
5. egg
6. bird

Activity 2, page 8

1. children
2. Heaven
3. holy
4. God's
5. good
6. needs
7. merciful
8. grace
9. hears, strength
10. greater

Activity 3, page 9

Jesus is the **Son** of God.
He came down from **Heaven**.
Christmas is Jesus' birthday.
Her name is **Mary**.
God gave Jesus a **foster** father.
Jesus came to **save** all people from their sins.
Jesus came to bring God's **love**.

Activity 4, page 10

Order of numbers:
8, 1, 5, 6, 2, 4, 3, 9, 7

Activity 5, page 11

"Jesus" means "God saves".

Activity 6, page 12

Activity 7, page 13

the other Mary
angel
happy
Jesus
embraced
"**Do** not be **afraid**."

Activity 8, page 14

cross, see, dove, fire, Church

Activity 10, page 16

1. pope
2. bishops
3. priests
4. deacon
5. holy
6. marry

Activity 11, page 17

water, prayer book, candle

Activity 12, page 18

Yes, Yes, No, Yes

Activity 13, page 19

altar
vestments
Mass book
host
candles

Activity 14, page 20

(Any or all of these answers is correct.)
I see: 1, 2, 3, 4, 5, 6, 7, 8
I hear: 3, 4, 6, (possibly 1)
I touch: 2, 4 (possibly 7, 8)
I taste: 2
I smell: 1 (possibly 7)

Activity 15, page 21

mortal
Reconciliation
one hour
food
Communion
Word
Eucharistic Prayer
"Amen"

Activity 18, page 25

1. Obeyed His parents.
2. Helped the sick.
3. Loved children.
4. Prayed.
5. Gave people food.
6. Told people about God's love.
7. Loved people whom others did not like.

Activity 19, page 26

1. 3
2. 1
3. 2
4. 2

5. 1
6. 3

Activity 20, page 27

1. 8
2. 5
3. 10
4. 4
5. 7
6. 6
7. 9
8. 4
9. 8

Activity 21, page 28

1. c
2. b
3. d
4. e
5. a
6. f
7. g
8. h

Activity 22, page 29

1. Both
2. My family
3. Holy Family
4. Both
5. Holy Family (possibly both)
6. Both
7. My family
8. Both

Activity 24, page 32

1. C
2. D
3. A
4. B

Activity 25, page 33

The hidden letters, in order top to bottom, are ADORE.

Activity 27, page 36

Yes

Answer Keys

Activity 30, page 40
1. e
2. g
3. i
4. j
5. h
6. k
7. a
8. l
9. d
10. f
11. c
12. b

Activity 33, page 43
1. e
2. b
3. f
4. c
5. d
6. g
7. i
8. h
9. a

Activity 34, page 44
1. Father, heaven
2. Son
3. Holy Spirit, Mary
4. crucified
6. third
7. right
8. dead
9. believe, Church, saints
10. sins, life

Activity 35, page 46
1. Father
2. consubstantial
3. for us men and for our salvation
4. Pontius Pilate
5. was crucified, suffered death, was buried
6. the Scriptures
7. seated at the right hand of the Father
8. in glory
9. Who with the Father and the Son is adored and glorified.
10. The Prophets.
11. one, holy, catholic, apostolic
12. baptism

13. the resurrection of the dead, the life of the world to come

Activity 37, page 48
1. Omnipotent: All-powerful, almighty, having unlimited power
2. Omniscient: All-knowing, having infinite knowledge
3. Sovereign: Reigning independent of others, above or superior to others, ruling
4. Holy: Spiritually perfect, without sin
5. Just: Right or fair, impartial, upright, lawful, correct
6. Everlasting: Without end, eternal, existing through all time
7. Wise: Having good judgment, making right choices, discerning
8. Faithful: Steadfast, loyal, reliable, dependable, true
9. Good: Virtuous, excellent, pure, correct, desirable

Activity 38, page 49
1. generous
2. kind
3. generous
4. just
5. life-giving
6. wise
7. kind
8. just
9. merciful
10. holy

Activity 39, page 50
1. powerful
2. good
3. knowing
4. male, female, image

Activity 40, page 51
Adam—Sixth
Fish—Fifth
Day—First
Night—First
Eve—Sixth

Stars—Fourth
Trees—Third

Activity 41, page 52
1. False
2. True
3. True
4. True
5. True
6. False
7. True
8. False
9. True
10. False

Activity 42, page 53
1. Saint Michael the Archangel
2. Guardian angel(s)
3. Gabriel

Activity 43, page 54
1. Son
2. Adam
3. Lord
4. Risen
5. Bread
6. Lamb
7. Man
8. Good
9. I Am
10. Light

Activity 44, page 55
1. Pentecost
2. Apostles
3. Mary
4. Abraham
5. Church
6. Holy Spirit
7. water
8. Scripture
9. dove
   The name Jesus used for the Holy Spirit is PARACLETE.

Activity 45, page 56
love
joy
peace
patience
kindness
goodness
faithfulness
gentleness
self-control

Activity 46, page 57
1. O (H)
2. A
3. O (C)
4. H
5. C
6. H
7. O
8. C
9. A
10. H
11. C (O)
12. A

Activity 49, page 61
1. Uncle Henry
2. a. serious (mortal) sin
   b. fast
3. Increases our union with Christ, renews grace from Baptism, removes venial sin, strengthens us against future sin, strengthens our love of God and neighbor, unites us to one another, reminds us of the poor
4. At least once a year (during the Easter season)
5. As often as he is properly disposed and attends Mass, even daily. Communion may be brought to the sick who cannot attend Mass.
6. Because of its link to the Last Supper that Jesus shared with his Apostles, at which he instituted the Eucharist
7. We re-create Jesus' one sacrifice on the Cross. The Eucharist makes present the one true sacrifice.
8. The words of institution or consecration
9. All of our blessings, including forgiveness of sins, redemption, and Christ's sacrifice

Answer Keys

10. The priest
11. Adoration, private Holy Hours, Benediction, Exposition of the Blessed Sacrament, bringing of Communion to the sick

Activity 50, page 62

1. P
2. G
3. W
4. R
5. P
6. G
7. R
8. W
9. P
10. R
11. W
12. R
13. W

Activity 51, page 63

1. T
2. T
3. F
4. T
5. T
6. T
7. T
8. F
9. F
10. T
11. F
12. T

Activity 52, page 64

1. b
2. c
3. a
4. c
5. c
6. b
7. c
8. a
9. b
10. a
11. a
12. c

Activity 54, page 66

1. Pray each day.
2. Go to Mass.
3. Read the Bible.
4. Love one another.
5. Obey parents.
6. Teach children.
7. Celebrate together.

Activity 55, page 67

Honor your **father** and your **mother**. "that your days may be long in the land which the Lord your God gives you."

Activity 56, page 68

First Commandment: I, the Lord, am your God . . . you shall have no other gods besides me.
Second Commandment: You shall not take the name of the Lord your God in vain.
Third Commandment: Remember the sabbath day, to keep it holy.
Fourth Commandment: Honor your father and your mother.
Fifth Commandment: You shall not kill.
Sixth Commandment: You shall not commit adultery.
Seventh Commandment: You shall not steal.
Eighth Commandment: You shall not bear false witness against your neighbor.
Ninth Commandment: You shall not covet your neighbor's wife.
Tenth Commandment: You shall not covet your neighbor's house . . . or anything that is your neighbor's.

Activity 57, page 69

Deuteronomy
1. Brought them out of the land of Egypt, freed them from slavery, led them toward the promised land.
2. To use his name carelessly or as a curse word, to fail to show proper awe and reverence when using God's name.
3. God made it holy because he rested from his labor of creating the world on the seventh day.
4. Yelling angry, mean things at someone; wishing harm upon someone in one's thoughts; hitting.
5. Tell a lie, talk about someone behind his back, gossiping.
6. "Covet" means to desire enviously something that belongs to someone else. Covetousness makes us angry at God and others, and unhappy and ungrateful with what God has

given us. It can lead to other sins, such as adultery, stealing, or killing.

Activity 58, page 70

1. choose
2. obey
3. inner
4. Spirit
5. Commandments
6. ignorance
7. evil
8. sin
9. Church
10. love

Activity 63, page 75

1. Petition
2. Thanksgiving
3. Praise
4. Blessing and adoration
5. Thanksgiving
6. Intercession
7. Blessing and adoration
8. Praise
9. Intercession
10. Petition

Activity 64, page 76

2. After the Lord's Prayer, *petition*
3. Preparation of the Gifts, *blessing/ adoration*
4. General Intercessions (Prayers of the Faithful), *intercession*
5. Penitential Rite (Lord, Have Mercy), *petition*
6. Eucharistic Prayer (Preface), *thanksgiving*
7. Glory to God, *praise*
8. Breaking of the Bread (Lamb of God), *petition*
9. Preface acclamation (Holy, Holy, Holy), *blessing/adoration*
10. Eucharistic Prayer (concluding acclamation), *praise*

Activity 66, pages 79–80

1. a. Jesus calls himself the "Good Shepherd" in the Gospel (Gospel of John).
   b. His sheep!
   c. I don't always know where I'm going and am in need of guidance; God cares for me and protects me from danger, and so on.
   d. Peaceful, hopeful, content, assured, safe.

Answer Keys

2. a. Anguished, distraught, suffering, hopeless
    b. Jesus' crucifixion. Verses 7–11, 15, 16, 18–19
    c. Accept any answer.
3. a. Praise (or blessing/adoration)
    b. Assembly. Addresses the people of God: Sing to the Lord a new song . . . Give to the Lord you families of nations, and so on.
    c. Glory, wondrous deeds, great, highly to be praised, awesome, splendor, majesty, grandeur, king, made the world, governs with equity, rules with justice, constancy

Activity 67, pages 81–82

Activity A
1. e
2. p
3. c
4. l
5. q
6. g
7. b
8. r
9. o
10. k
11. i
12. n
13. h
14. t
15. d
16. m
17. s
18. j
19. f
20. a

Activity B
Connecting the dots spells "Mary".

Activity C
1. The Baptism in the Jordan; Luminous
2. The Resurrection; Glorious
3. The Annunciation; Joyful
4. The Agony in the Garden; Sorrowful

Activity 70, page 86
1. follow, Apostles
2. Pentecost
3. Commandments
4. novena
5. Beatitudes

6. sacraments
7. created, nothing
8. Pentateuch, laws
9. Matthew, Mark, Luke, and John
10. Father, Son, and Holy Spirit
11. descendants, Adam, Eve, Eden
12. True God

Activity 71, page 88
1. d
2. b
3. c
4. j
5. c
6. a
7. f
8. k
9. a or b
10. e
11. g
12. d, f, j

Activity 73, page 91
1. h
2. d
3. g
4. b
5. c
6. g
7. a
8. f
9. e
10. b

Activity 74, page 92
1. d
2. b
3. e
4. g
5. a
6. f
7. c
8. h

Activity 75, page 93
1. needs food
2. is one
3. has many parts
4. is organized, designed by God
5. is connected, interrelated
6. grows
7. has a head
8. is beloved
9. is pure, beautiful
10. is cherished, cared for
11. is God's building
12. is holy

13. is a dwelling place of God
14. is built upon the foundation of the apostles, prophets, Christ
15. has a (precious) cornerstone

Activity 76, page 94
1. poverty, chastity, obedience
2. hermits
3. virgin
4. religious
5. set apart
6. missionary
7. the world
8. Church
9. example, witness

Activity 78, page 98
1. death of the body (dead)
2. resurrection
3. Baptism
4. particular judgment
5. heaven
6. purgatory or purification
7. hell
8. last judgment
9. new heaven, new earth

Activity 79, page 99
1. h
2. e
3. k
4. a
5. p
6. m
7. b
8. l
9. q
10. n
11. c
12. j
13. f
14. g
15. i
16. o
17. d

Activity 80, page 100
1. Mt 8:8, Lk 7:6–7
2. A centurion, a Roman army officer
3. To heal his servant from sickness
4. That he has the power to heal with just a word
5. Yes
6. No. He comes into my mouth (my body) in Holy Communion

Answer Keys

7. To heal my soul of sin (or sickness, meaning spiritual sickness)
8. Humility and trust (or faith, love)

Activity 83, page 103
1. April 7
2. December 25 *
3. November 24
4. December 1
5. December 8 *
6. May 26
7. May 16
8. January 7
9. February 21
10. April 5
11. November 1 *
12. August 15 *
13. March 17
14. December 29
15. January 1 *
16. March 25
17. June 9
18. June 2
19. September 8
20. June 14

Activity 84, page 105
1. b
2. c
3. c
4. a
5. a
6. c
7. a
8. b
9. a
10. b

Activity 85, page 106
1. Baptism, Confirmation
2. Baptism
3. Anointing of the Sick
4. Any or all four
5. Baptism, Confirmation
6. Holy Orders

Activity 87, page 108
1. love
2. consent
3. dissolved
4. faithful
5. word
6. trial marriages
7. grace
8. Christ
9. children
10. life

Activity 88, pages 110–111
Activity A
Accept any reasonable answers.
Examples:
1. By praying we come to know God better; we become more confident that he is there.
2. When we ask God for help in our weakness, we often find new sources of strength, giving us even more trust in God than we had before.
3. We are never more happy than when we are giving of ourselves to others. We often find that we want to give even more.

Activity B
1.	T	9.	T
2.	F	10.	P
3.	J	11.	T
4.	P	12.	P
5.	J	13.	T
6.	J	14.	F
7.	F	15.	J
8.	P	16.	P

Activity 90, page 114
Across
2. circumstances
4. good
8. intention
9. sin
10. emotions
11. free
Down
1. responsible
2. conscience
3. actions
5. object
6. means
7. firm

Activity 92, page 118
1. A
2. C
3. F
4. I
5. J

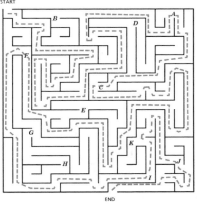

Activity 93, pages 120–121
1. Accept any reasonable answer, including legalized abortion, growing acceptance of "assisted suicides" and incidents of euthanasia, cases of infanticide.
2. Accept any reasonable answer.
3. Accept any reasonable answer, including healings, the raising of Lazarus, his ultimate sacrifice on the Cross, and the fact of the Incarnation, in which Christ became man.
4. Should be permitted only if absolutely necessary for the protection of society; modern prison security makes need for death penalty all but obsolete.
5. Natural law, Sacred Scripture, Tradition of the Church, Magisterium.
6. Killing of an innocent, helpless child at request of the child's own mother, who by nature should nurture and protect her child.
7. Suffering can be offered to Christ for remission of sins of self or others; can increase one's identification with Christ, who suffered on the Cross; can encourage others if endured bravely; and so on.

Answer Keys

8. b and c
9. Accept any reasonable answer.

Activity 94, pages 121–122

Activity A
A. 5
B. 6
C. 9
D. 8
E. 4
F. 2
G. 1
H. 7
I. 3

Activity B

1	9	2	4	5	7	6	8	3
5	3	7	1	6	8	9	4	2
6	8	4	3	2	9	7	1	5
2	1	8	7	9	4	5	3	6
7	4	3	6	1	5	8	2	9
9	6	5	2	8	3	4	7	1
4	5	1	8	3	6	2	9	7
8	2	6	9	7	1	3	5	4
3	7	9	5	4	2	1	6	8

Activity 95, page 125

1. Accept any answer.
2. Accept any answer.
3. Receiving praise helps me to know myself, to love myself, and to recognize that I am created in the image of God.
4. Giving praise helps me to look for the good in others and to recognize that they are created in the image of God. Giving praise is a way to love others. To love someone for his own sake and not for any benefit to myself should be the motive for giving praise.
5. Flattery is untrue or insincere praise. It is against the Eighth Commandment because it is a form of deceit. Flattery is usually given in order to obtain something from someone.

6. Giving correction can sometimes be a moral duty when the soul or welfare of another person is at stake. It is also the responsibility of those with authority—such as parents, teachers, pastors, and civil leaders—who teach, train, or govern others. The motive for giving correction must always be love of the person for his own sake, that is, concern for his welfare.

Activity 97, page 127

1. G
2. H
3. J
4. E
5. K
6. I
7. A
8. B
9. C
10. D
11. F

Activity 98, page 128

1. Through Christ we are God's children.
2. Christians are brothers and sisters in Christ.
3. Accept any reasonable answer.
4. That he make his name holy, or that he glorify his name.
5. For Jesus Christ to return in glory and judge the world.
6. That we love one another as he has loved us.
7. Physical and spiritual.
8. The Eucharist.
9. To share our bread with the hungry; to receive Holy Communion; to bring Communion to those unable to attend Mass.
10. Accept any reasonable answer that relates the forgiveness we ask of God to the forgiveness we grant others, even enemies.
11. The Holy Spirit
12. He keeps us from being tempted beyond our strength and gives us a way out to avoid sin.
13. Satan.

Activity 99, page 129

1. Verse 1; the hour of his death
2. Verse 20
3. Judas Iscariot
4. b
5. d
6. a
7. c

NOTES

NOTES

NOTES